OLD-TIME COUNTRY GUITAR BACKUP BASICS

Based on commercial recordings of
the 1920s and early 1930s
by Joseph Weidlich

First Opry tour group, 1930. Standing, Kirk McGee, Dr. Humphrey Bate, Dorris Macon, Buster Bate, Aclyone Bate, Lou Hesson. Seated, Sam McGee, Uncle Dave Macon.

Layout and notation by Ken Warfield

ISBN 1-57424-148-6
SAN 683-8022

TABLE OF CONTENTS

BIOGRAPHY

Joseph Weidlich [b. 1945] began his formal musical studies on the classic guitar. He moved to Washington, D.C. in 1972, from his native St. Louis, to teach classic guitar. He performed in several classic guitar master classes conducted by notable students of Andres Segovia (i.e., Sr. Jose Tomas [Spain], Oscar Ghiglia [Italy] and Michael Lorimer [U.S.]). He has also played renaissance guitar, renaissance lute, and baroque guitar.

In 1978, he completed research on and writing of an article on *Battuto Performance Practice in Early Italian Guitar Music (1606-1637)*, for the Journal of the Lute Society of America, 1978 (Volume XI). This article outlines the various strumming practices, with numerous examples, found in early guitar methods published in Italy and Spain in the early 17th century. In the late 1970s he published a series of renaissance lute transcriptions for classic guitar, published by DeCamera Publishing Company, Washington, D.C., which were distributed by G. Schirmer, New York/London. The American Banjo Fraternity published an article Joe wrote on James Buckley's *New Banjo Book* [1860] in their newsletter, the *Five-Stringer*, #185, Double Issue, Fall-Winter 2000-01.

The banjo has also been no stranger in Joe's musical life. He began learning folk styles in the early 1960s during the folk music boom, later playing plectrum and classic banjo styles as well. His extensive research in the history of minstrel banjo demonstrates how that style formed the foundation of clawhammer banjo. Alan Jabbour, noted old-time fiddler, musicologist and former long-time director of the Library of Congress' American Folklife Center, has said of Joe's book, *The Early Minstrel Banjo: Its Technique and Repertoire*, that "our understanding of the minstrel banjo in the 19th century is greatly enhanced by the long labors you have devoted to the subject and the fine understanding you have brought to it."

Joe has collaborated with banjo builder Mike Ramsey (Chanterelle Workshop, Appomattox, Virginia) in designing two prototype minstrel banjos based on the dimensions described in Phil Rice's *Correct Method* [1858], as well as similar instruments made by William Boucher in Baltimore in the 1840s.

Also published by Centerstream Publishing are Joe's editions of a flatpicking guitar edition of George Knauff's *Virginia Reels* [1839], believed to be the only substantial extant compilation of nineteenth-century Southern fiddle tunes published prior to the Civil War (which includes songs later featured in the early minstrel shows), *Minstrel Banjo—Brigg's Banjo Instructor* [1855], *More Minstrel Banjo-Frank Converse's Banjo Instructor, Without A Master* [1865], *Guitar Backup Styles of Southern String Bands from the Golden Age of Phonograph Recordings*, which features the guitar backup styles of Ernest Stoneman's Dixie Mountaineers, the Carter Family, Charlie Poole and the North Carolina Ramblers, Gid Tanner and the Skillet Lickers, and Jimmie Rodgers, often acknowledged as "the father of country music" and *Painless Arranging for Old-Time Country Guitar*.

A BRIEF INTRODUCTION TO "OLD-TIME MUSIC"

No form of "country music," a term first coined in the 1940s, existed in 1923, the year of the waxing of a conservative 500 copies of the first "country" music recording, made by 50-year old Fiddlin' John Carson of Atlanta, Georgia. At that time there was no existing market in the South to merchandise a style of music that did not originate in New York's Tin Pan Alley. In fact, with the exception of the music publishing companies the music industry as we know it today didn't really exist at that time, thus it grew up side-by-side with the recording era (which had began about the turn of the century) and the development of the radio in the 1920s.

While the growing availability and low cost of purchasing gramophones in urban areas led to the manufacturing of more and more recordings there were no recordings specifically marketed to the population of the South, who had just begun to be able to afford to purchase these players from their local furniture stores (where gramophones, wax cylinders and 78s were usually sold in those days). The unexpected recording success of Fiddlin' John Carson led to the for-

John Carson, with his daughter Rosa Lee.

mation of a new record series: one marketed for Southern whites and another for marketed African-Americans (even though it was common practice for African-Americans and Southern whites to play music together and trade licks).

Record company executives realized that it would not be practical to provide transportation to a large number of potential artists located throughout the South to travel to New York or Chicago to make recordings in front of the then current technology, the recording horn (and the great physical bulk of archaic recording machinery associated with that technology). It is fortuitous that at about that same time that the electric microphone had just been introduced by Western Electric, which made the concept of remote recordings possible as the equipment could be now transported by automobile. It wasn't long before recording company producers began to set up field studios in furniture stores, hotels or warehouses in many Southern locales. In this way, many more local groups could be recorded and, if record sales warranted, be invited to record additional songs in professional studios. One of the most famous of these remote recording sessions was the one held in Bristol, Tennessee, in 1927, where producer Ralph Peer searched for "authenticity" in the playing of songs, old or new, in the traditional manner.

Who were these performers whose music led record companies to market their music as "old time" or "old familiar tunes"? They certainly were not professional musicians, by any means. They were primarily unschooled simple folk, in many senses of the word, using very basic musical accompaniments to the tunes they knew how to play at home for themselves or local social functions. They were happy to just receive the extra money for recording their "sides" of music that they played to supplement their meager income.

In the rural setting of the South the singing of old songs was often unaccompanied. When music was played away from the home it tended to be for dancing or some kind of contest. The "core" instruments used were usually the fiddle and banjo, where the banjo "seconded" the fiddle. This style goes back to the early 19th century minstrel show [ca. 1843] whose standard instrumentation were the fiddle, banjo, bones and tambourine.

Fiddle. The principal instrument of the old-time music genre was the fiddle, seemingly always the lead instrument. The fiddle served several functions: to provide dance music, to provide accompaniment to the voice, or solo fiddle music without a particular social function, e.g., for their own enjoyment.

The fiddle was particularly important in accompanying vocal music as it could be used to imitate, i.e., "double" the vocal line, thereby reinforcing the primary contours of the melody or to provide ornamentation, based on the melodic line. As the melodies of the songs became simpler, in the sense of using less vocal ornamentation, the fiddle style likewise became simpler. This transition was aided by the addition of the banjo and guitar, which provided additional decorative elements, thus freeing the fiddle to focus primarily on lead melodic functions.

Banjo. Besides the fiddle, the mountain banjo was the most important ensemble instrument, as it was used to reinforce the main notes of the melodies played by the fiddle. The banjo introduced a steady, strong rhythm to maintain the beat, so important when playing for dances. In fact, the clawhammer banjo style, in particular, was, and still is, highly regarded for this role.

While the 19th century minstrel banjoists traditionally used two basic tunings (what today would be equivalent to the natural C tuning and open G tuning) an interesting feature of the Southern mountain banjo was the development of several additional tunings to suit the modal character of the traditional melodies being sung and played. Scholars seem to think that these systems of altered tunings may have been worked out by the turn of the 19th century, perhaps influenced by open guitar tunings needed for playing certain parlor guitar songs (e.g., the Spanish fandango) and the beginning of the African-American blues guitar styles. These modal melodies would then be accompanied on the banjo so that the principal melodic notes could be played without the need to play harmonic chords or shift up and down the fingerboard, whose chord voicings would not be practical most of the time playing in these altered tunings (the newly introduced guitar would now supply this harmonic accompaniment). Occasionally, the banjo was used as a solo instrument on early commercial recordings (e.g., by Charlie Poole using fingerstyle techniques); however, its usual role was to support the fiddler.

Charlie Poole

Guitar. While guitars had been available in the United States for most of the 19th century, principally in urban industrialized areas, e.g., by C.F. Martin, Ashborn, S.S. Stewart, and Washburn, by the end of that century guitars were beginning to become available in even greater numbers, aided in part by a much improved mass transportation system, the advent of the industrial revolution, and mail-order houses like Sears Roebuck. In the last decade of that century the guitar was gaining rapidly in mass popularity due to its usage in mandolin bands, glee clubs, and university banjo bands, thus not just for use in its traditional 19th century environment, the parlor.

String Bands. From the 1920s, with the introduction of the guitar into the string band ensemble, the emphasis, at least in terms of recording, shifted from providing music for dances to the accompaniment of vocal songs and fiddle tunes. That necessarily changed the function of the string band instruments, freeing up the ensemble for various duties. The guitar was now used to mark out the harmonic structure of the song, that is, provide the bass function by playing low bass note runs during chord changes and marking out the major rhythms, thus providing a regular rhythmic structure to hold the band together. Every good band had its own distinctive sound, and the guitar backup style contributed to that sound.

Repertoire. The old-time repertoire consisted not only of songs familiar from earlier generations such as traditional old-time ballads, music from gospel songbooks, and 19th century parlor songs (songs that had gone into the folk tradition transformed, perhaps, by revised or new lyrics), but also popular songs, music hall songs, dance tunes, fiddle tunes, event songs (e.g., train wrecks, mining disasters) and even genuine folk ballads (such as *John Hardy* and *Tom Dooley*).

The Depression killed record sales and those who recorded music, particularly the "old time" artists. Strings bands would not be recorded again until the late 1930s, by which time musical tastes had changed. That decade began to be influenced by radio and movies: cowboys playing guitars (Gene Autry and Tex Ritter), the new western swing band format of Bob Wills or Sons of the Pioneers, radio barn dances (Chicago's National Barn Dance and Nashville's Grand Old Opry), and "brother acts" like the Monroe's, Stanley's, Delmore's, and Red Sky Boys.

The string band format and instrumentation would be "updated" by Bill Monroe and his Blue Grass Boys in the 1940s, which would lead to a new style of music eventually called bluegrass.

Post-War Rediscovery. By 1952 extended playing [EP] long playing [LPs] records were just being introduced, so one could listen to a number of different selections in a row instead of a one at a time, as with 78rpm or 45rpm records. That year saw the release of a curious mixture of songs on six extended play records containing 84 songs covering traditional ballads, social music, and songs. The artists were not contemporary; in fact, after hearing the archaic sounds presented on these records many buyers assumed that the artists were dead, "had to be." This was the famous Folkways collection called the "Anthology of American Folk Music", edited by Harry Smith (frequently referred to as the Harry Smith Collection or Harry Smith Anthology). The performances were unauthorized reissued copies of the original 78s made by the artists of the late 1920s and early 1930s. While this collection is considered the "founding document of the American [urban] folk revival" of the mid-1950s, it is a fact that these songs were still being played in the South, even by the same artists, but by now long forgotten! A new generation of avid urban music listeners were in shock hearing this non-Tin Pan Alley/Broadway/big band music that came from an entirely different age and culture.

Fortunately, today you can easily obtain compact discs of this original material from a variety of record labels such as Yazoo, Document, County Sales, the Library of Congress, the Smithsonian Institution, etc. The only difference is that today these old timers are, indeed, deceased.

INTRODUCTION

Welcome to the world of old-time country guitar. This book will focus on examining the standard backup techniques used by string band guitarists who recorded in the 1920s and the early 1930s, specifically those who used a thumbpick (we will adapt their techniques to today's flatpick style) versus blues guitarists, who adapted the classic fingerstyle techniques used to play the parlor guitar.

Most of the old-time country guitar backup techniques are based on three very basic things: [1] the boom-chick pattern (alternation of a bass note and a block chord, as the index, middle and ring fingers were used to play the first three strings as a unit); [2] bass runs connecting chord changes; and [3] use of the pentatonic scale. With a solid foundation in those basic techniques presented in this book, you will find that by just adding very slight variations to them you will have sufficient knowledge and technique to hold your own in backing up fiddle tunes, etc., in the old-time traditional country guitar style.

The final part of this book focuses on some interesting variations on these basic backup licks, which I transcribed from commercial string band recordings of the 1920s and early 1930s.

In order to use this book most efficiently you should know how to read guitar tablature, know how the major scale is constructed, which of those scale degrees make up a major chord, and basic chord progressions. This information is easily accessible from many sources and easy to learn, particularly as many of the songs in the old-time country repertoire use only the I, IV and V chords.

Let's get started having some fun!

PART ONE

BACK-UP BASICS

Brothers Kirk and Sam McGee.

LESSON 1
BOOM-CHICK PATTERNS

The song that I will be using throughout the first part of this book in helping you develop your backup techniques is entitled *The Little Old Cabin in the Lane*. This song was written in the years immediately following the Civil War. Here it is written out in guitar tablature and staff notation:

The Little Old Cabin in the Lane

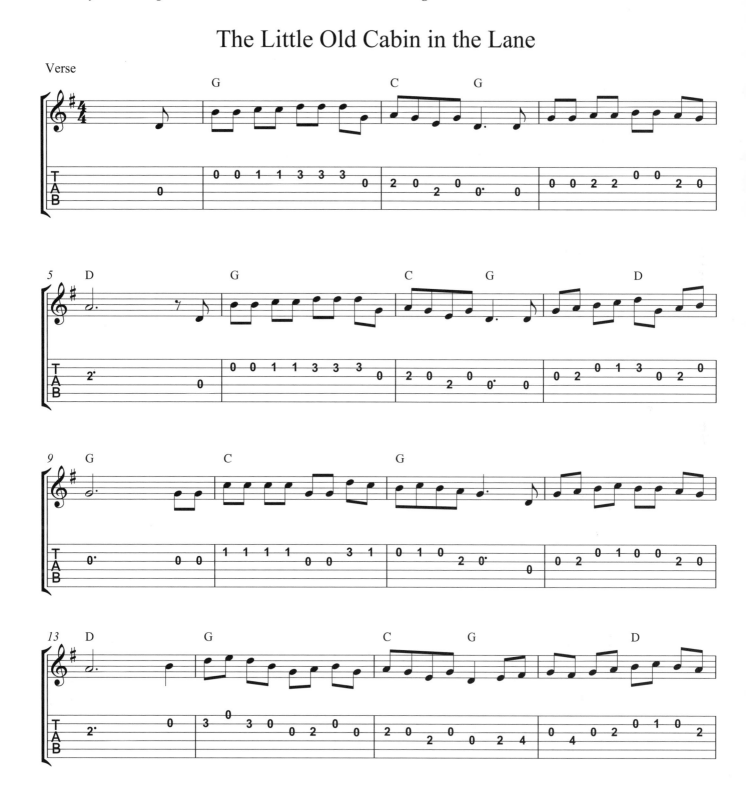

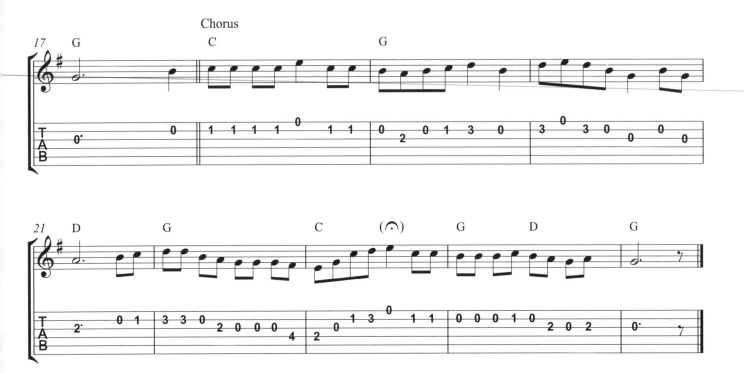

The first thing that you will need to do is to learn the melody, the chord changes (G, C and D for this song) and where these changes occur in the song. This does not mean memorizing the song note-for-note but just getting used to how the song sounds and where the harmony changes, so you know when to change chords. Since the song is written in Common time (also called 4/4 time), where there are four quarter notes or their equivalent per measure, I suggest that you initially play just the correct root of the chord on each beat. Example #2 demonstrates this single note Root usage:

Example #2

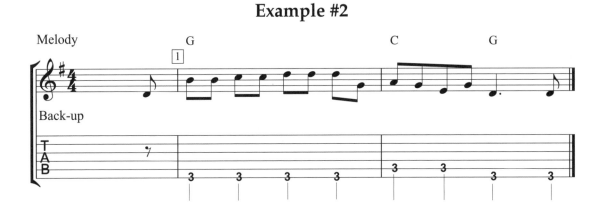

Once you are comfortable doing this, the next step is to add a strum in between those Root notes (this note-strum sequence is traditionally referred to as a "boom-chick" pattern). It was common for the string band guitarists to play this way when backing up (that is, providing accompaniment) songs at a fast tempo. It is still a popular technique today in bluegrass guitar backup.

String band guitarists usually used a thumbpick and their index, middle and ring fingers as a unit to play the boom-chick pattern. The thumb played the bass notes while the fingers were used to play the first three strings as a single block of notes, together. If you try this you will see that the notes played by the thumb, if you use a thumbpick, are far louder then those played by the fingers. Thus, we should try and emulate this to the extent feasible in our backups, as there is a distinct sound between strumming three strings or more than three strings.

Since we are using a flatpick, the most basic way is to use a <u>light</u> <u>down</u> <u>stroke</u> for the strum, where possible. (Of course, if you wish to use the original thumbpick-finger approach, go right ahead and do so.) Thus, you play the bass note with a downstroke, preferably having the pick land on the next lower string (called a rest stroke), then playing the first three strings as a unit with the flatpick, starting with the third string. If the tempo is too quick to do this, then use an upstroke beginning on the first string for the strum.

Here is a brief boom-chick pattern for the first two measures of *The Little Old Cabin in the Lane* written out:

Example #3

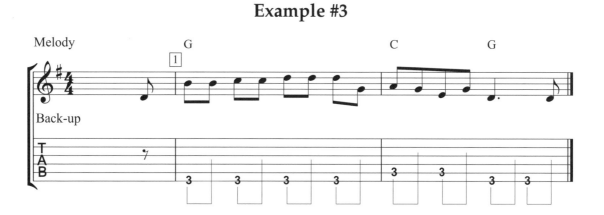

Wilf Carter - Montana Slim.

11

LESSON 2
ALTERNATING BETWEEN ROOT AND FIFTH OF A CHORD

The usual bass notes used in the boom-chick backup patterns are the Root, third and fifth of the chord. Let's start by using just the Root and fifth of the chord. Normally, the Root is played on the first and third beats and the fifth on the second and fourth beats. Thus, you will alternate between the G and D notes in the G chord, the C and G notes in the C chord, and the D and A notes in the D chord.

You will notice if you do this for *The Little Old Cabin in the Lane* that you will occasionally play the same Root note twice in a row, for instance, the G note when going from the C chord to the G chord in the second measure. This is all right. For those measures of C [measures 2, 6 and 14] you could just as easily play the G first, then the C. A similar note duplication can be found at measures 7 and 23, when the G chord moves to the D chord.

The standard Root-fifth backup is written out for you in Example #4:

Example #4

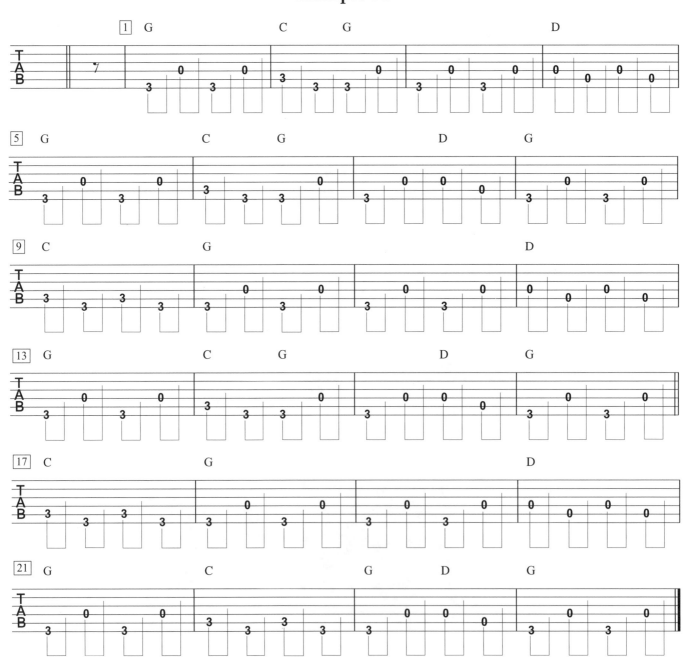

When you are comfortable doing this, move ahead to Lesson 3.

LESSON 3
6-7-8 BASS RUN CONNECTORS

Now that you are getting comfortable alternating between the Root and fifth of the chords in your backup it is time to introduce bass runs to connect chord changes. The use of rest strokes are preferred when playing these types of runs to emphasize the harmonic change.

Bass runs can move up <u>or</u> down to the Root of the next chord; however, ascending seems to be the usual pattern. The lead-in notes are usually the two diatonic notes below [6-7] or above the Root [3-2] of the next chord [see Lesson 6].

Right now, let's work on the 6-7-8 bass run, so named because its usage is based on the 6th, 7th and 8th scale degrees of the tonic major scale (the 8th is the Root of the tonic chord, one octave higher). For instance, in changing chords from G to C in the first measure of *The Little Old Cabin in the Lane*, the arrival note, C, is on the first beat of the second measure, so the lead up notes, the 6th and 7th (the A and B notes, respectively, which are really the 2nd and 3rd scale degrees of the G major chord but in this case act as 6-7) are played on the fourth beat of the first measure as a pair of eighth notes.

Here are two examples of 6-7-8 bass run connectors:

Example #5

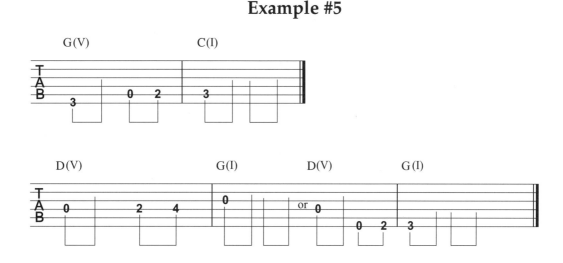

Bass runs do not have to be used every time that there is a chord change. For instance, when a phrase is repeated where the same chord change occurs you may choose to, for instance, continue using boom-chick patterns instead of using a bass run connector. This is your choice.

The concluding note of the 6-7-8 run is usually the Root of the arrival chord; however, that note could just as easily be the 7th of a V7 type chord. Here is an example of that type of movement:

Example #6

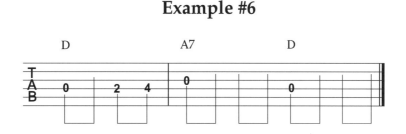

LESSON 4
GOLDEN AGE LICK

I would now like to discuss what I call the Golden Age Lick, which is a distinctive-sounding musical phrase often used by old-time country guitarists at the end of songs. The Golden Age lick often begins on the fourth beat of the penultimate measure in the guise of a standard 6-7-8 connector bass run, arriving on the Root note of the arrival chord on the first beat of the final measure, <u>then repeated</u>, which reinforces the arrival and stability of the tonic chord.

For instance, here is how you could use this lick in measures 23-24 of *The Little Old Cabin in the Lane*:

Example #7

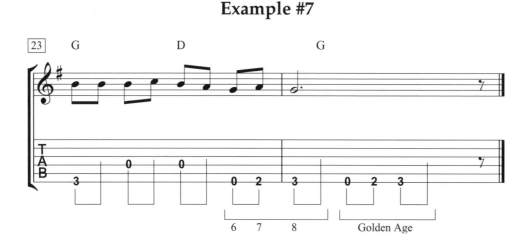

The 6-7-8 note sequence is very handy as it can also be used as a substitute/variation for a standard boom-chick pattern:

Example #8

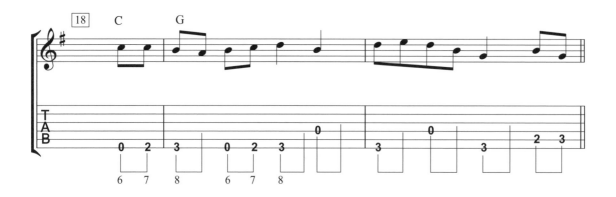

14

Example #9 is a backup arrangement of *The Little Old Cabin in the Lane* using the techniques discussed so far. Note that in this backup I occasionally shift the placement of the Root and fifth, which I briefly touched on in Lesson 2.

Example #9

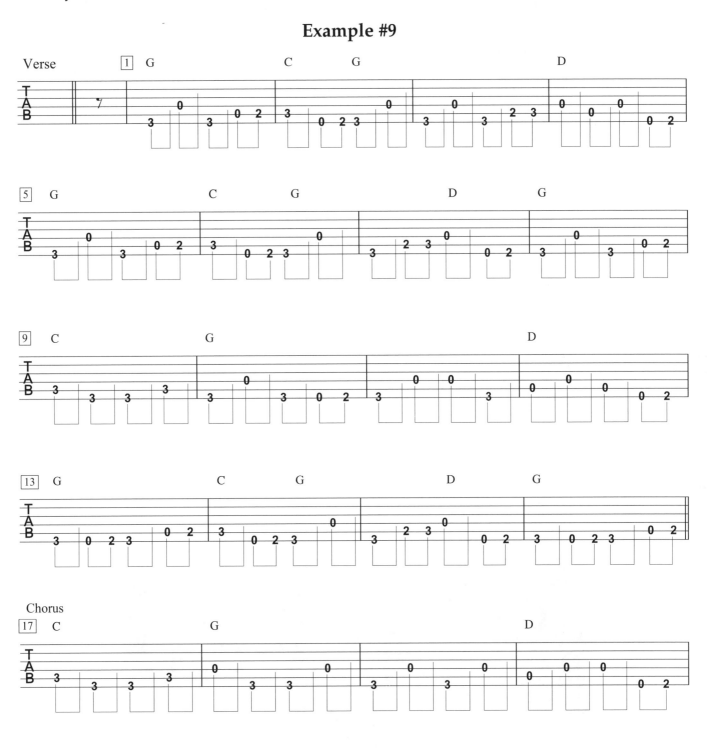

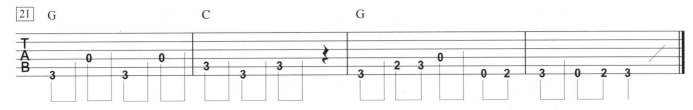

LESSON 5
THE THIRD OF THE CHORD IN BACKUPS

It is now time to introduce the third of the chord in our alternating bass boom-chick patterns. Because the use of the third fills in the larger intervallic distance between the Root and the fifth we now have the ability to create smoother, melodic-sounding backups. You will find that <u>the</u> <u>sound</u> of the boom-chick patterns will change; when used in connection with the 6-7-8 or 3-2-1 bass note connectors you will have many more opportunities to expand the melodic shape of the accompaniment.

Example #10 shows the use of the third in measures 1-8 of *The Little Old Cabin in the Lane*:

Example #10

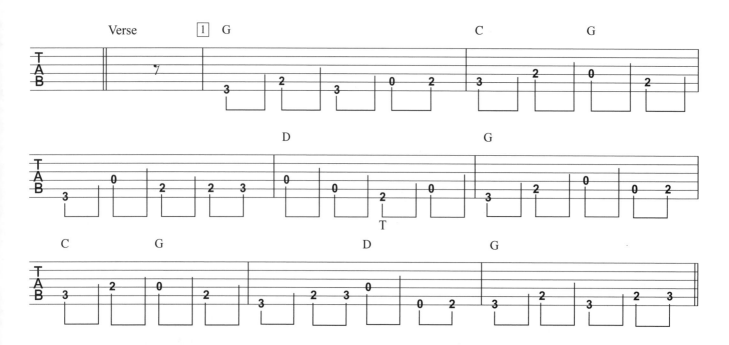

John McGhee and Frank Welling, circa 1928.

LESSON 6
3-2-1 BASS RUN CONNECTOR

In Lesson 3, I mentioned that the 6-7-8 ascending note sequence could be replaced by a descending 3-2-1 note sequence (inverted sequence of 6-7-8), also played twice in succession. For instance, the 6-7-8 note sequence of E, F sharp to G, used to arrive at the key of G (6-7-8), can instead be replaced by B, A to G [3-2-1]. Likewise, in the key of D, F#-E-D (3-2-1) can be used instead of the standard 6-7-8 connector notes of B-C#-D.

Example #11

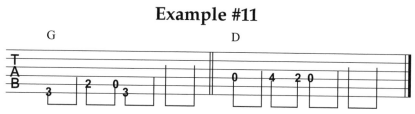

Try this out in measures 23-24 of *The Little Old Cabin in the Lane* instead of the standard boom-chick pattern or the 6-7-8 bass run connector shown in Example #9.

Example #12

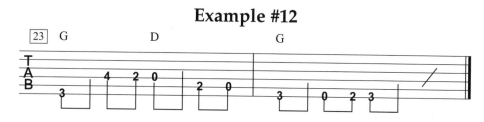

The 3-2-1 bass run connector can also be played twice in succession, as in the Golden Age lick. Here is an example in key of D:

Example #13

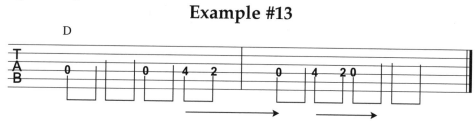

Although I prefer to follow the traditions of the string band guitarists in using the 6-7-8 Golden Age lick to end a song, here is an example of the fiddle tune *Whiskey Barrel*, which uses the 3-2-1 connector lick to end the song:

Example #14

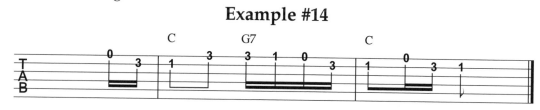

The 6-7-8 and 3-2-1 note sequences can also be mixed: play one, then the other. Again, it can be used in measures other than cadences, sometimes played in one entire measure, in others crossing a bar line. Here is an example:

Example #15

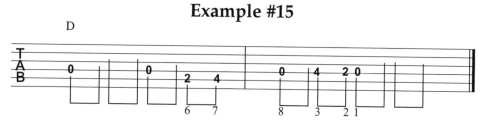

LESSON 7
PENTATONIC SCALE

The pentatonic scale is used quite frequently in old-time country guitar backup. This scale consists of the Root, second, third, fifth and sixth degrees of the diatonic major scale. For instance, in the key of G, these notes are G, A, B, D and E.

Example #16

It is precisely because neither of the half-steps of the major scale are used in the pattern (that is, between scale steps 3-4 or 7-8, which have a motion/leading-tone resolution function) that makes the pentatonic scale neutral in character, thus able to be seamlessly fitted into standard backup patterns.

If you are familiar with bluegrass guitar you will notice that this scale sounds familiar because it serves as the basis for the Lester Flatt G-Run. Later on in this book I will show a number of examples of that usage in old-time country guitar backup.

More often than not, the second note of the scale is not used in old-time guitar backup when using the scale in a descending motion, thus allowing the scale to fit into two beats with resolution to the Root on the following beat. Thus, it fits nicely into the existing Root-third-fifth standard backup alternating bass patterns. It is usually most effective if the root of the pentatonic scale is the target arrival note. Here are two examples of a pentatonic scale, one in C and one in G.

Example #17

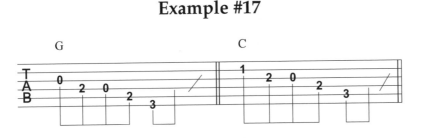

Here are some examples of the pentatonic scale with pick-up notes:

Example #18

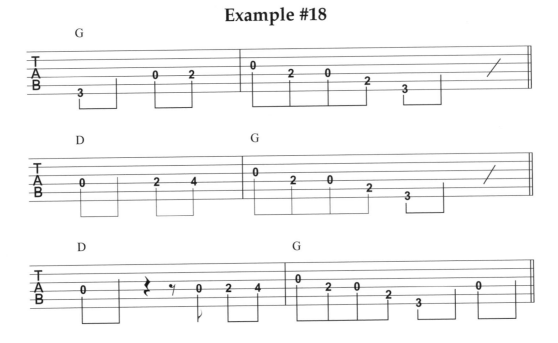

18

Instead of 8-6-5-3-R, a short note sequence of 6-5-8 can be substituted. Here is an example:

Example #19

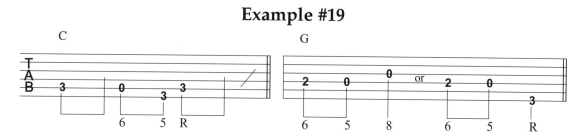

Delta blues guitarist Charlie Patton frequently used a **5-6-8** short-note sequence in his slide guitar playing; guitarist Charlie Monroe also used it in his recordings with his brother, Bill, in 1936.

Now, here are two examples using the pentatonic scale in the verse of *The Little Old Cabin in the Lane* (measures 5 and 13):

Example #20

===========================

Congratulations! You now have the ability to create a standard old-time country guitar backup arrangement, using many of the basic idiomatic techniques found in many of the classic string band recordings of the 1920s and early 1930s. Let's build on this firm foundation and have even more fun as you develop your backup skills.

LESSON 8
ASCENDING AND DESCENDING TRIAD USAGE

We have been using the Root, third and fifth in our backup style (the use of the third was introduced in Lesson 5) and also as the final three notes of the descending pentatonic scale (see Example #17).

Let's now introduce the use of triads, that is the Root, third and fifth notes of the major scale, which in G are the G, B and D notes; in C, the C, E and G notes; and in D, the D, F# and A notes. These three chords are the I, IV and V chords respectively in the G major scale, and the notes of each chord are part of the diatonic G major scale.

When using the Root-fifth alternation, the third fits naturally on the offbeat returning to the Root, thus a descending triad figure.

Example #21

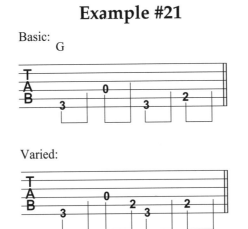

Here is an example where the fifth and third are placed on the <u>fourth</u> <u>beat</u> of a measure:

Example #22

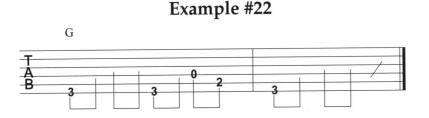

Here are some typical ascending triad figures:

Example #23

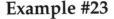
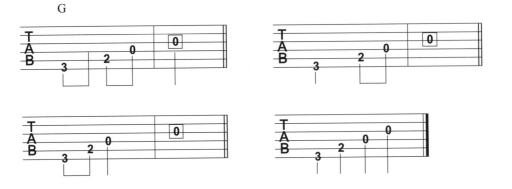

Here is an example of the use of a dotted eighth note in a descending pentatonic scale:

Example #24

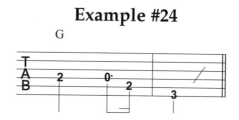

Here is an example of a triad used in a V-I cadence figure:

Example #25

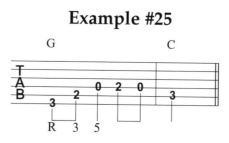

Now, here is an example of how you might use triads in the chorus of *The Little Old Cabin in the Lane*:

Example #26

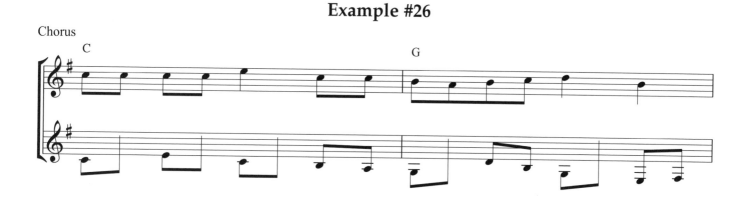

LESSON 9
REINFORCE MELODIC LINE

It is not uncommon for old-time country guitarists to reinforce the main melody notes, particularly in instrumental numbers such as fiddle tunes or ragtime tunes and, in particular, blues songs, where the guitar often plays the notes of the melody as it is sung. This doubling can be done several ways: one way is to play just the on-the-beat melody notes found in a particular measure; another is to play a complete measure of the song as presented instead of a standard backup measure; a particularly effective way is to play part of the melody an octave lower or higher, where possible.

Here is one way you could reinforce the melody line in measures 1-4 of *The Little Old Cabin in the Lane*:

Example #27

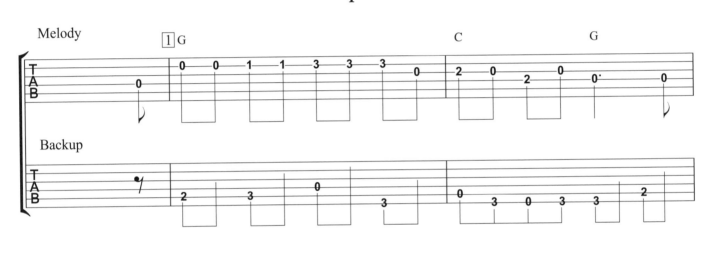

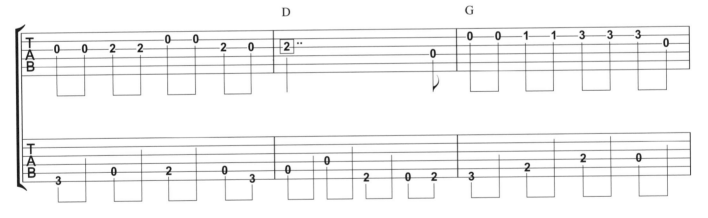

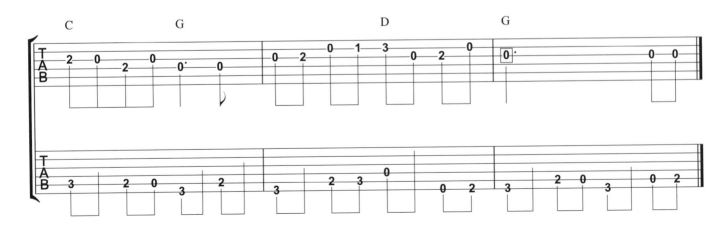

22

LESSON 10
SCALES

You can also use short scale runs for any of the standard backup techniques or substitutions, such as a "lick" for a certain chord. For instance, instead of a standard boom-chick for the C chord, play some kind of scale fragment. Here is how it could work in measures 20-21 of *The Little Old Cabin in the Lane*:

Example #28

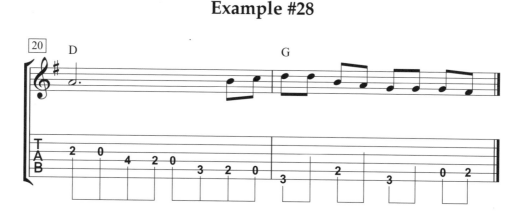

LESSON 11
CHORD PROGRESSION LICK

This is a substitution lick you can use to replace, for instance, a series of basic boom-chick patterns and/or bass run connectors over a basic chord progression, for instance, D to G [V to I]. Here are two examples: the first was a favorite of Henry Whitter (of Grayson & Whitter fame) [this lick would fit nicely in measure 4 of *The Little Old Cabin in the Lane*]; the second is one used by the Carter Family.

Example #29

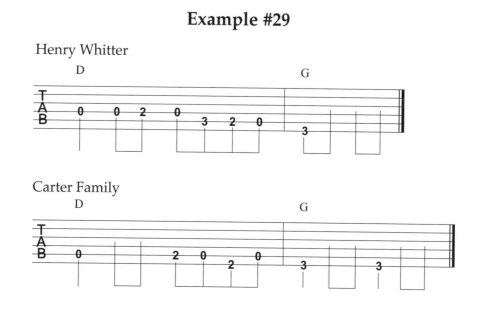

LESSON 12
5-6-7-8 BASS RUN CONNECTOR

The 6-7-8 bass run connector can be extended by adding the fifth note of the scale to the run, either on the weak beat of the third beat (as the fourth beat is where the 6-7 notes of the bass run connector usually begins) or by playing the fifth twice in succession, taking up the entire third beat of a measure. Here is how these might be used in measures 1-2 of *The Little Old Cabin in the Lane*:

Example #30

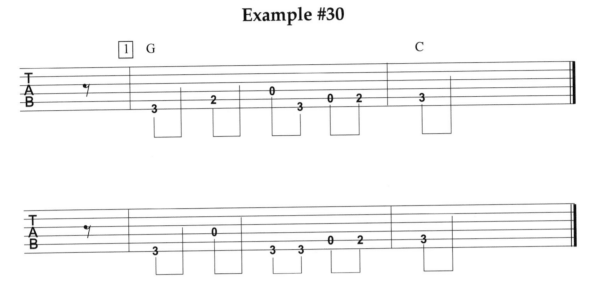

Occasionally, pedal tone notes are introduced in the 5-6-7-8 connector lick, thus creating a series of 16th notes. Here is one such example:

Example #31

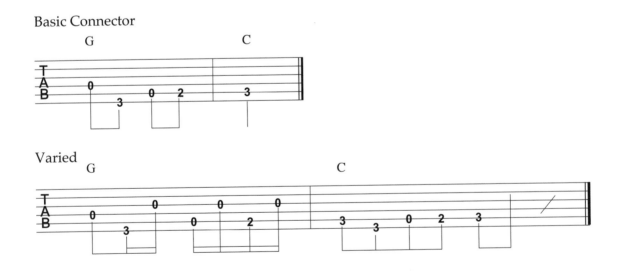

LESSON 13
VARIED GOLDEN AGE LICK

The fifth can also be added to the Golden Age lick. In the four examples below, note the mixture of the standard 6-7-8 and 5-6-7-8 bass connector notes.

Example #32

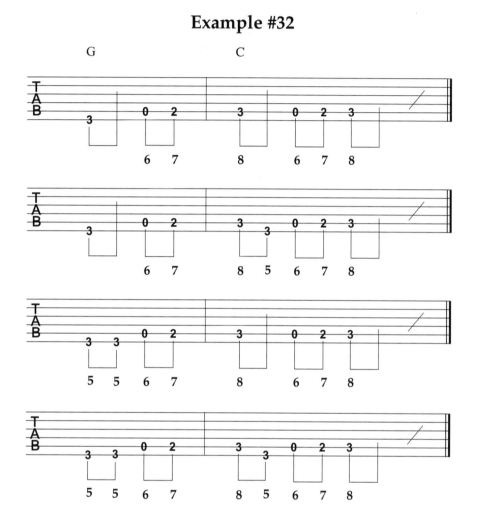

The use of the fifth brings up an interesting point in transcribing music from historic recordings. For instance, if the fifth is used, then the guitarist was probably playing out an A chord position as the fifth is not available in the key of G because the open sixth string, E, is the sixth note of the G major scale.

LESSON 14
LEADING TONE FUNCTIONS

In Lesson 8 I mentioned that in the key of G the I, IV and V chords were G, C and D, respectively. The 6-7-8 bass run connector notes used for those chord changes are those found in the G major scale: G-A-B-C-D-**E-F#-G**. The intervallic distance between the seventh and eighth notes, F# to G, is a half-step. This particular forward motion is called, in music theory circles, the leading tone, i.e., the seventh note <u>leads</u> you to the tonic of the scale, in this case G.

In the G, or I, chord, the F# leads to G; in the C, or IV, chord, the B leads naturally to C. In the D chord, however, the 6-7-8 connector run is B-C-D; thus, the seventh note, C, is a whole step below D instead of the half-step leading tone function, C# (this whole step distance on the seventh scale degree is called the subtonic). In cases like this, feel free to raise the seventh note one half step. Likewise, you may choose to alter the leading tone note by lowering it one half step to a sub-tonic, or flatted seventh, function. Roy Harvey, guitarist with Charlie Poole and the North Carolina Ramblers, frequently used this technique in his guitar backups.

Here is an example of an altered leading tone function in measures 7-8 of *The Little Old Cabin in the Lane.*

Example #33

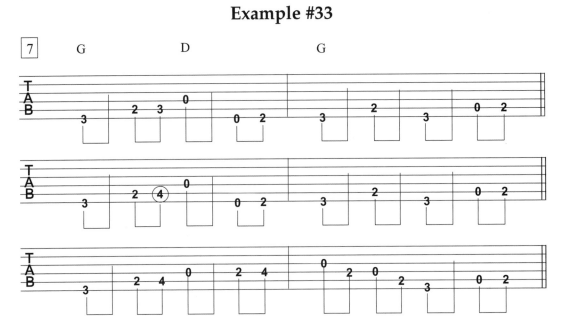

The leading tone function can also be used to replace a weak beat strum in a boom-chick pattern to create a quasi-leading tone before a chord change. Here is how it might be used in measure 14 of *The Little Old Cabin in the Lane.* Again, Roy Harvey used this technique a great deal in his playing.

Example #34

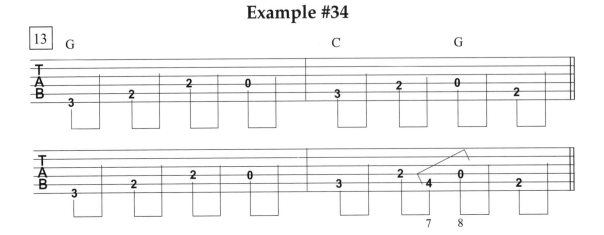

LESSON 15
CONCLUDING THOUGHTS

You may have noticed, if you already play guitar, that some common idiomatic guitar techniques, such as hammer-ons, pull-offs, slides, and arpeggiated rolls, etc., have not been presented. While these were techniques commonly used by country blues guitar players from that chronological time period, those techniques are not used all that often in old-time country guitar backups, per se. There are a few examples, usually by guitarists who played in jug bands in the Memphis area, which will be shown in Part Two. There doesn't seem to be any particular reason for this lack of usage as, for instance, they were commonly used by the Carter Family in their many recordings, as well as Riley Puckett, who played guitar with Gid Tanner and the Skillet Lickers. These "missing" techniques seem to become more commonly used by guitarists who began recording in the late 1930s, a time when the string band format was undergoing several changes for a variety of different reasons.

Now, here is a backup arrangement of *The Little Old Cabin in the Lane* using many of the techniques discussed so far in this book.

Example #35

The Little Old Cabin in the Lane

Chorus

28

The Little Old Cabin in the Lane

Tab Version

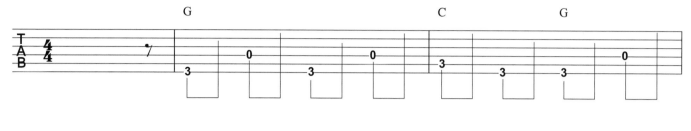

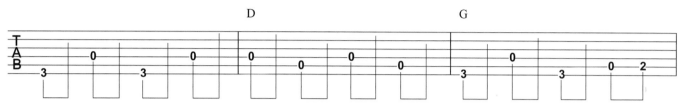

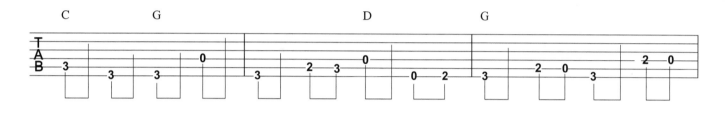

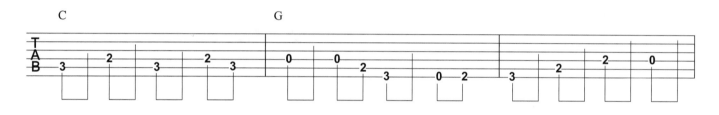

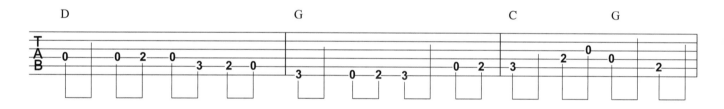

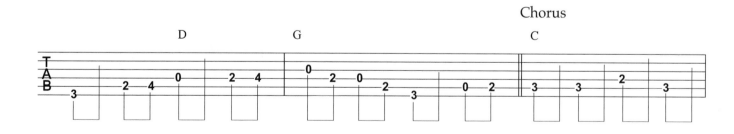

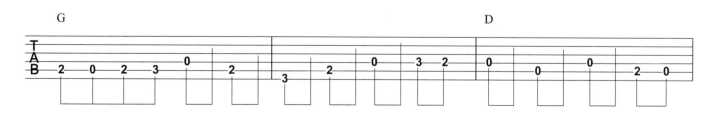

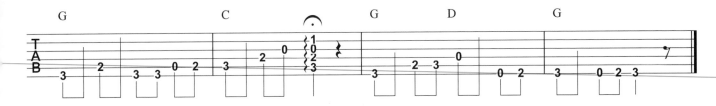

Well, that's it. With the material presented in Part One, you can develop interesting backup accompaniments for old-time country guitar songs, bluegrass guitar, or folk music. When you consider how many of these techniques can be substituted for each other it should be apparent that you have a wide variety of opportunities at your disposal. The important thing is to get used to using them, particularly understanding <u>why</u> they are used where.

The remainder of this book will be devoted to various old-time country guitar licks, most of which are just variations of the basic techniques which you have already learned here. Enjoy reading through them, and put them to use in your backup arrangements.

Have fun!

PART TWO

EXAMPLES FROM THE REPERTOIRE OF OLD-TIME COUNTRY GUITARISTS AS COMMERCIALLY RECORDED IN THE 1920s AND EARLY 1930s.

Memphis Minnie.

Welcome to Part Two of *Old-Time Country Guitar Backup Basics*. In this section of the book I will present variations on the basic techniques presented in the Part One of this book. The bracketed number above the treble clef sign refers to the song title and artist from which the example was extracted (see Song Reference List).

The following techniques will be covered in this part:

Backup Techniques: Basic boom-chick patterns
                            Use of interval of a third
                            Connector notes
                            Leading Tone function

Pentatonic Scale

Lester Flatt "G runs"

Chromatic Passing Tones

Licks: Licks based on a chord
                       Chord Progression Licks

Use of 16th notes: Pickup notes
                            Scale runs

Miscellaneous: Hammer-ons
                            Carter Family style
                            Rolls
                            Triplets

The Stanley Brothers.

BACK-UP TECHNIQUE

Let's begin our survey of guitar backup techniques by looking at some examples of the basic boom-chick pattern. Example 36 in C uses the standard alternating Root-fifth pattern, the phrase concluding with a 6-7-8 bass run connector (this example can easily be used as vamp chord progression), while Example 37 in G uses the alternating Root-third pattern, then a triadic outline in place of a standard boom-chick pattern.

Example #36

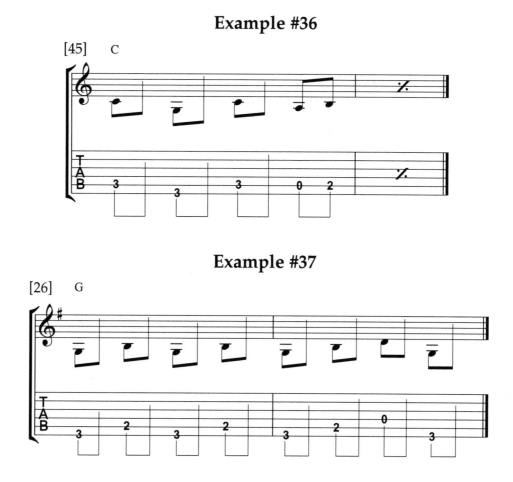

Example #37

Example 38 resembles Example 37 but uses a repeated root note in the boom-chick pattern, then the 6-7-8 bass run connector is used for the chord change. Note the octave shift on the last two beats in the concluding measure.

Example #38

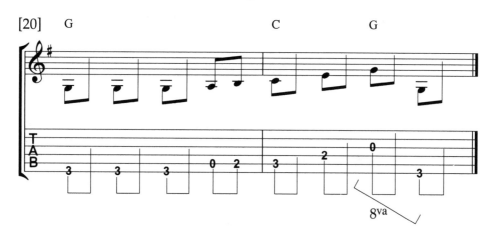

Example 39 in G is interesting in that it uses a strum on the downbeat of the fourth beat followed by a 16th note, which resolves to either the third or root of the G chord.

EXAMPLE #39

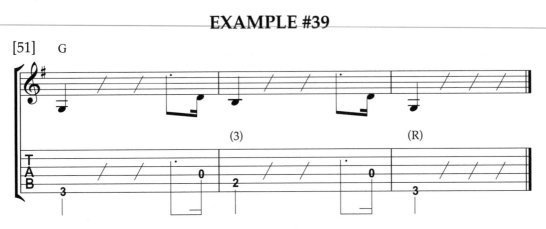

Example 40 demonstrates the use of the Root-third-Root on consecutive eighth notes. Here, I have also transposed it from the key of F to the key of G:

EXAMPLE #40

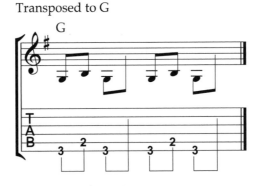

Transposed to G

Here is an example in G where the first three notes of the pentatonic scale are used. Note that the third note, D, is a common tone, that is, it is the root of the V chord as well as part of the G pentatonic scale. Also note the descending triad used to end the phrase.

EXAMPLE #41

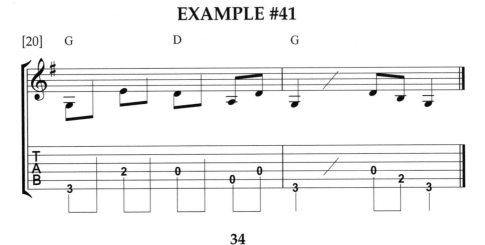

Example 42 in A outlines a triad for a full measure, not just to conclude a phrase. Also note the Root-second-third scale degree movement in the variation.

Example #42

Let's shift gears now and look at some examples demonstrating connector notes. Example 43 in C uses the 3-2-1 connector note sequence without a chord change, while the chord change from G to C (V-I) uses the 5-7-8 connector notes instead of the expected 6-7-8 connector note sequence.

Example #43

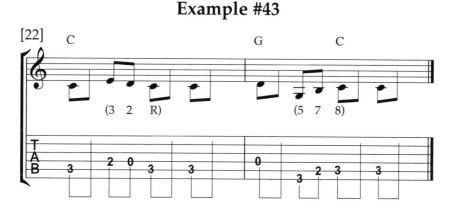

Occasionally, the first note of the 3-2-1 note sequence is flatted. This is a common device used by Riley Puckett in his playing with Gid Tanner and the Skiller Lickers. Here is an example from his playing in C:

Example #44

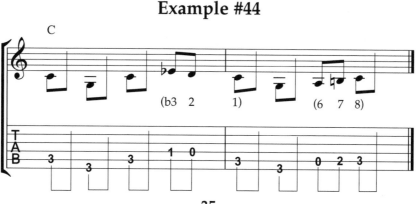

Examples 45 and 46 both use the 6-7-8 and 3-2-1 note sequence:

Example #45

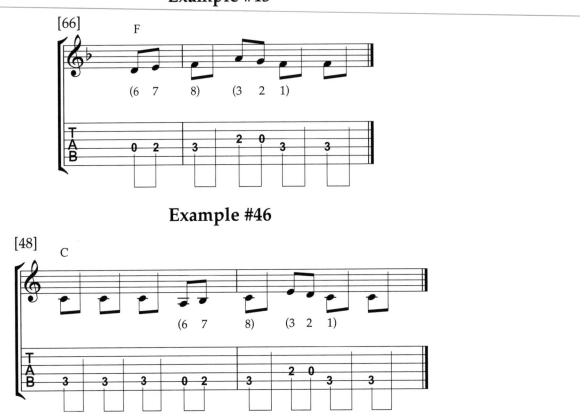

Example #46

Examples 47 and 48 in C both use the 5-6-7-8 note sequence. Note the dotted eighth note strum followed by the fifth to begin the connection.

Example #47

Example #48

Example 49 uses the 5-5-6-7-8 connection sequence. Note the use of the dotted quarter note on the first note of the run.

Example #49

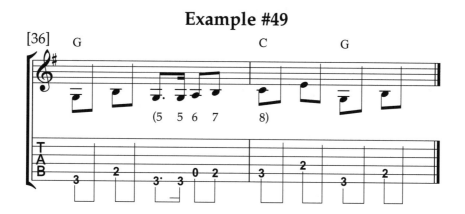

Here is an interesting example of a 6-5-8 note run in 3/4 time, which leads the IV chord [C] to the V chord [D]. Note the use of the triad (8-5-3-R) to end the phrase:

Example #50

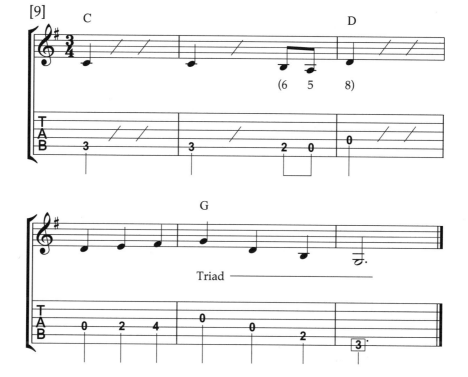

Example 51 uses the connector notes of 2-7-8, 3-2-1 and 3-5-R for this extended backup in G major.

Example #51

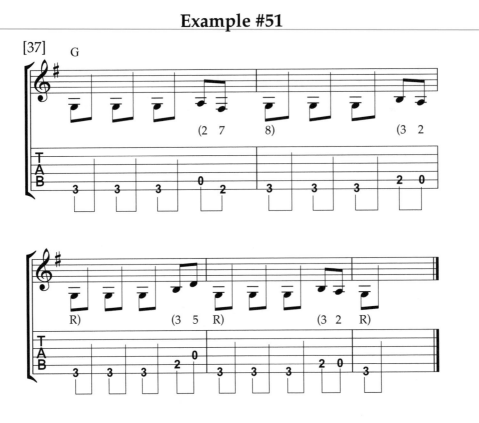

Here is an example I transposed from the key of F to G, which uses a 4-2-R note sequence. You could look at the C natural as the flatted seventh in D, followed by the fifth of D, A.

Example #52

Transposed from F:

Let's finish up this section on basic backup techniques by looking at some leading tone function ideas. In Example 53 you would ordinarily use a Root-third alternating bass pattern in C, which leads to a smoother melodic connection to D, the fifth of the G chord. However, in this instance the chromatic passing tone, C sharp, is used instead to connect C to D. This C#-D note sequence functions like the half-step leading tone function of a major scale. To play it, slide the third finger (along with the hand) up one fret from C to C#. You can then finger the G chord as you play the open fourth string, D. Note the two variations.

Example #53

Variation

Variation

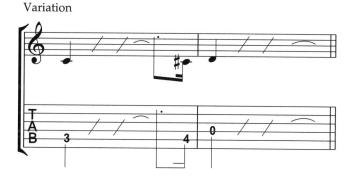

Example 54 displays a true natural leading tone function with an alternating bass note sequence over C major. This 5-7-8 note sequence was also used in Example 43.

Example #54

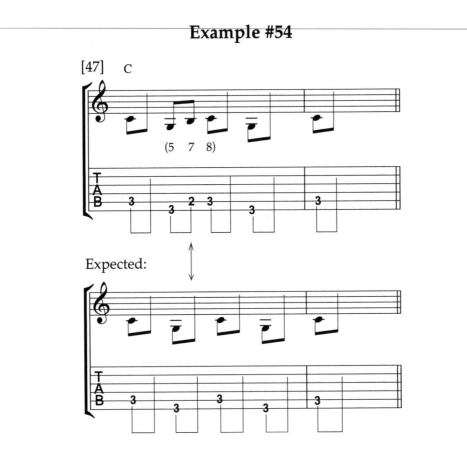

The 7-8 leading tone function is used in the next two examples. The note used as the leading tone in Example 55 has been chromatically raised one-half step because it is <u>not diatonic</u> to the C major scale.

Example #55

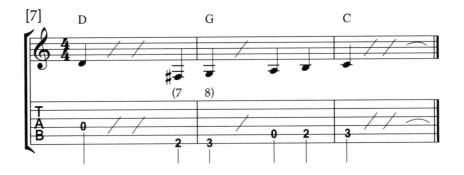

Example #56

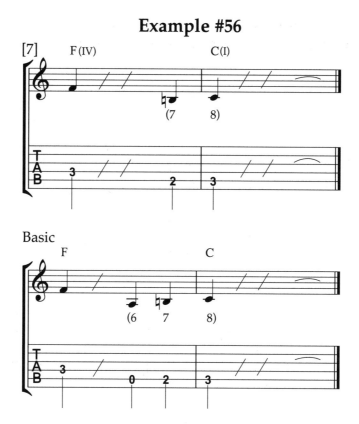

Let's move on to the pentatonic scale.

PENTATONIC SCALE

Example 57 outlines the pentatonic scale in a standard boom-chick pattern.

Example #57

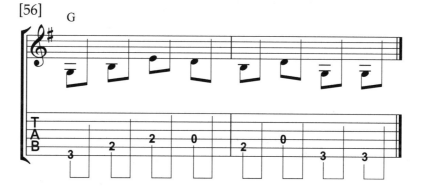

In Example 58, a slightly longer phrase, the basic pentatonic scale pattern is book-ended by a connecting scale.

Example #58

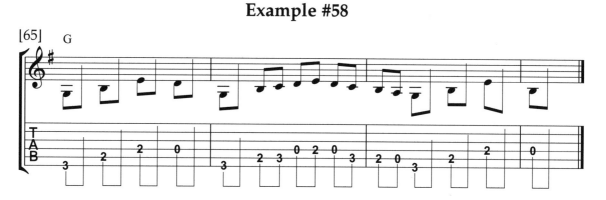

Examples 59 and 60 use the descending pentatonic scale note sequence. Note in particular the bass run connector used at the C-D chord change in Example 59, as well as the concluding Golden Age lick.

Example #59

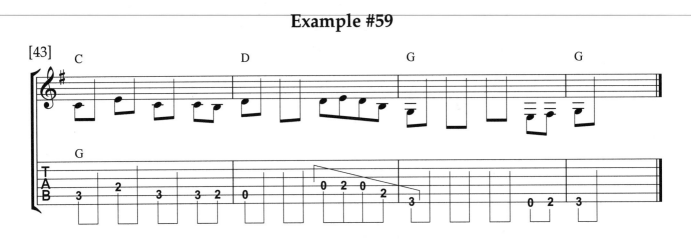

Example 60 begins with a 6-7-8 connector sequence. On the last two beats of the first measure the Root-third eighth note sequence leads into a 6-7-8 bass run connecting C to G. A leading tone function is also used on the second beat of the third measure, C# to D, followed by a scale which leads to the pentatonic scale run. Quite a lot is going on in these four measures!

Example #60

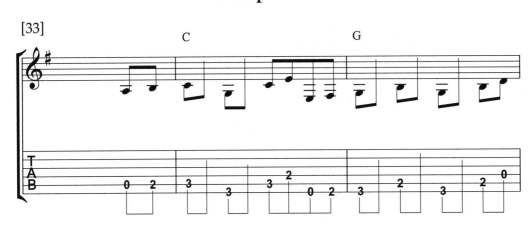

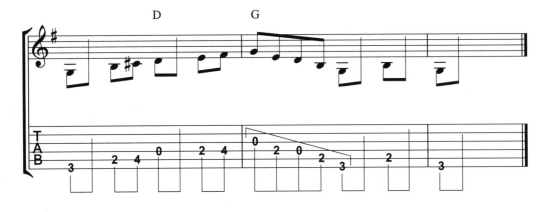

After the use of the 5-5 6-7 8 lead-in note sequence beginning Example 61, a substitute note is found in the descending pentatonic scale: the low E (open sixth string) replaces the expected third of the scale, B, then a slide is used to go to the G note on the sixth string.

Example #61

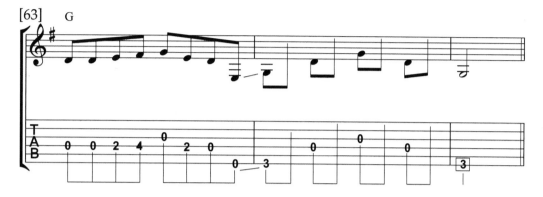

The next extract is based on a Major 6 chord, which is related to the pentatonic scale.

Example #62

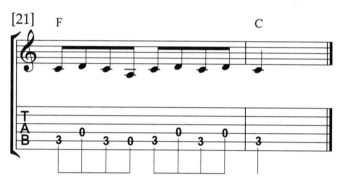

Extended:

Note at the end of this example the quarter notes C-D-E flat-E natural-C sequence and how those notes were used in the previous measure as eighth notes. I'll discuss this important note sequence/lick under Chromatic Passing Tones.

The final three examples use 16th note values for execution of the pentatonic scale, similar to the runs that Riley Puckett was famous for. Note in particular Example 65.

Example #63

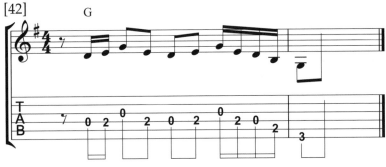

Example #64

Example #65

LESTER FLATT "G RUN"

In 1946, guitarist Lester Flatt, then a member of Bill Monroe's Blue Grass Boys, first recorded a kickoff lick on the song *Heavy Traffic Ahead* that would eventually be forever associated with his playing: the G run. This now famous run is based on the <u>ascending</u> note pattern of the pentatonic scale. However, the basis of this lick was not unknown in the recordings under study here. After laying out those extracts, I will provide a brief glimpse of its use by Bill and Charlie Monroe in their 1936 duo recordings.

The G run is based on the Root, third, fifth and sixth notes of the major scale. As the half-step intervals are not ordinarily used in this run, the pattern is pentatonic in nature.

Here is an example of the basic pattern. Note the use of the repeated notes.

Example #66

The next five examples are similar except that dotted eighth note usage is more prevalent.

Example #67

Example #68

Example #69

Example #70

Note in the following example how the run is used to go from the I to the I7 chord, i.e., G to G7:

Example #71

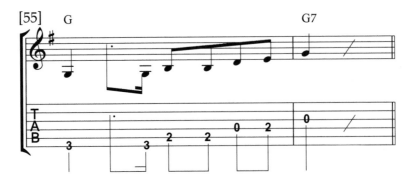

Here is an unusual example using the 16th note-dotted 8th note rhythmic pattern (traditionally referred to as the Scotch Hop) kicking off the run followed by a syncopated note pattern:

Example #72

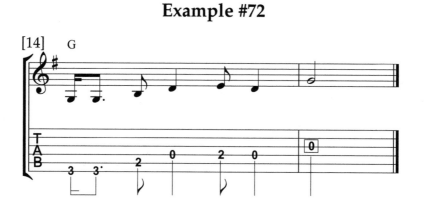

Here are two examples of a shorter note sequence somewhat identifiable to our ears today as a G-style run. In fact, the first example, the 5-6-8 run, was commonly used by blues guitarist Charlie Patton in his slide playing.

Example #73

Example #74

Here is a slightly extended use of the short note run, introduced by repeated notes. Note how a standard 6-7-8 bass run connector can be used instead (see optional measure).

Example #75

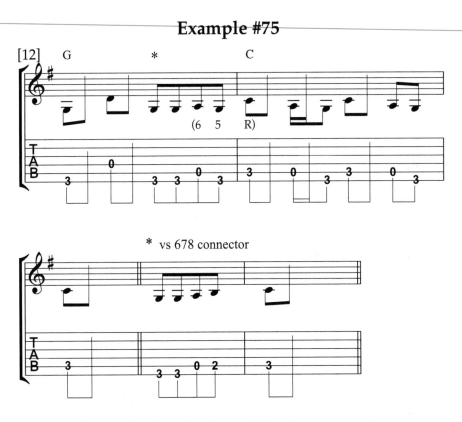

It is common to use the flatted third in the G run. Here is an example:

Example #76

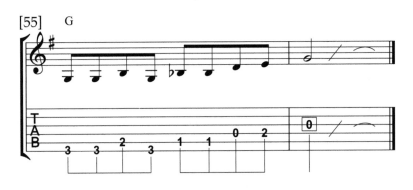

Here is an unusual example of the G run moving to the C chord, the I chord here:

Example #77

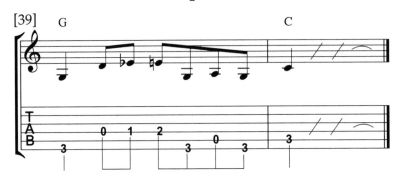

The G run can be used in keys other than G, or songs played out of the G position. For instance, here is an example in the key of E major:

Example #78

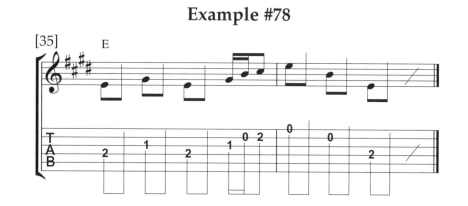

Irvin and Gordon Rouse

49

Here is an example of the leading tone of the G major scale, F sharp, used as part of the G run. I have included the entire back up here so that you can see the G run working in context.

Example #79

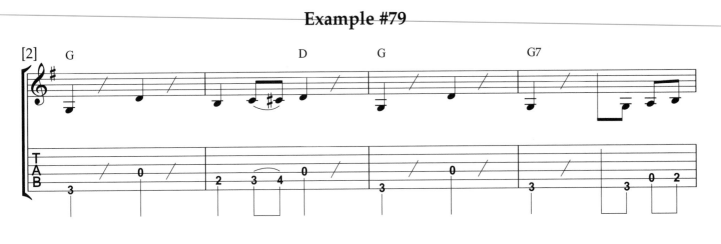

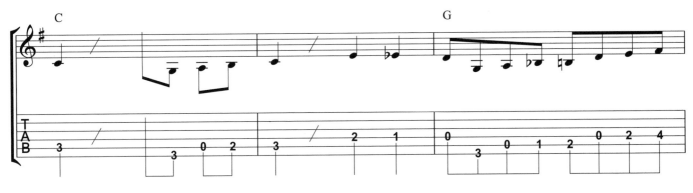

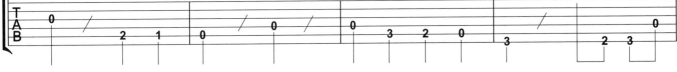

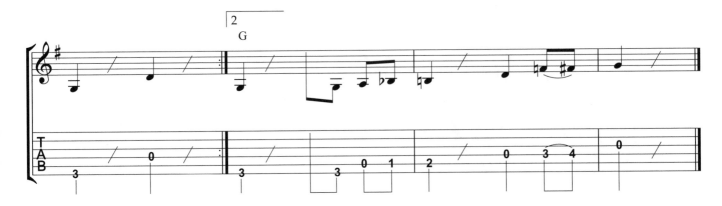

I want to now offer a few observations of the usage of this lick pattern by Bill and Charlie Monroe in the mid-1930s.

Bill Monroe established the "sound" of the G run in his mandolin recordings with his brother, Charlie, when he used it to either end his solos or to end songs. In fact, if you listen closely to those runs in the 1936 recordings the G run, the way we normally hear it today, is played only once, in the song *Darling Corey* (recorded June 21, 1936)! Let's look at some of the other ways it was being developed in those recordings.

Initially, Bill begins to establish this sound with a tremolo figure using a basic triadic figure.

Example #80

He then begins to expand on the notes used in the run:

Example #81

Next, he begins to experiment with the rhythm of those notes either by tying some of the notes or by dotting some of them. Here are some examples (note that Example 82 is based on the standard 5-6 7-8 connector note run):

Example #82

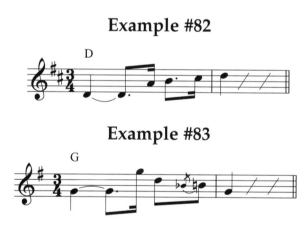

Example #83

Here are two examples where he begins to repeat notes in the run:

Example #84

Example #85

Here is an example of a descending G-style run.

Example #86

Next is an example where he uses the flatted third-natural third note sequence.

Example #87

Variation

Here is an example in which the leading tone is used in the run.

Example #88

Finally, here is the run used in *Darling Corey*:

Example #89

Charlie's standard guitar backup style is based for the most part on the material covered in Part One of this book. Since both he and Bill were using lots of pentatonic runs in their backups, they had to be careful not to tread on each other when using them. Thus, Bill often does not use the runs at all.

Here is an example of a short G run Charlie used in his backup:

Example #90

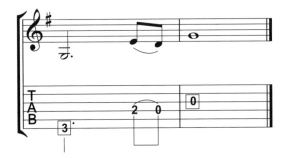

Well, that finishes my discussion on the Lester Flatt G run. I know that many of you will be somewhat surprised of its various guises and development by the Golden Age string bands years before Bill Monroe began to experiment with it to end phrases and songs in the mid-1930s.

Let's move on now to the important element of the use of chromatic passing tones as used on the historic commercial recordings of the 1920s and early 1930s.

CHROMATIC PASSING TONES

A very effective way to spice up your backups is to use the note that falls in between two adjacent notes a whole step apart, for instance, using C# to connect C to D. Here is an example:

Example #91

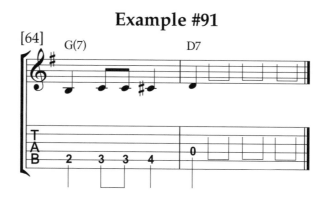

Next is an example where the first note of the 6-7-8 connector run, in this case, A, is <u>replaced</u> by the flatted seventh, B flat. The beat that was altered could just as easily have been a note-strum pattern.

Example #92

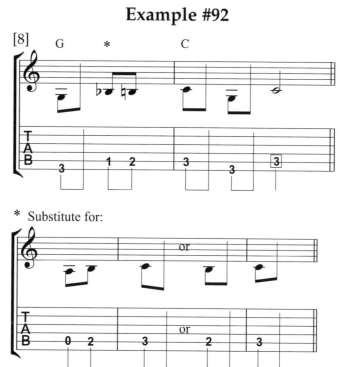

* Substitute for:

Since the principal blues notes of the major scale are the third and seventh, it is to be expected, borne out by many examples to follow in this section, that the natural third and seventh notes will often be altered. Here is a typical example in the key of G:

Example #93

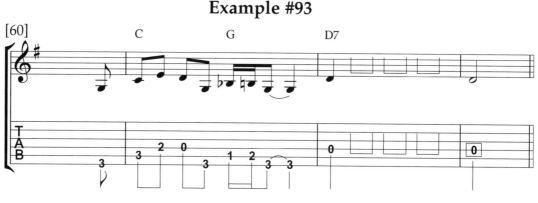

The next example is a little unusual as the chord progression is I-VI-V-I (C-A-G-C). To accommodate the root movement from C to A, a chromatic passing note (B flat) is used.

Example #94

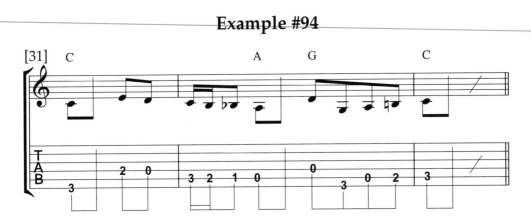

Here is a similar example in a longer musical phrase using a long series of individual notes (note the 3-3-2 rhythmic pattern in the second measure).

Example #95

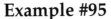

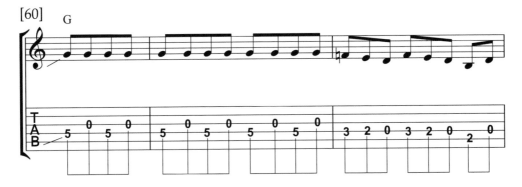

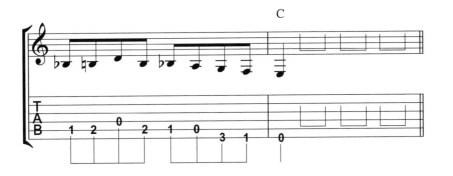

The next three examples each use a short run of chromatic notes:

Example #96

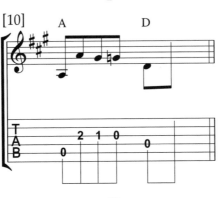

Example #97

Example #98

The next four examples focus on the use of the altered third scale degree:

Example #99

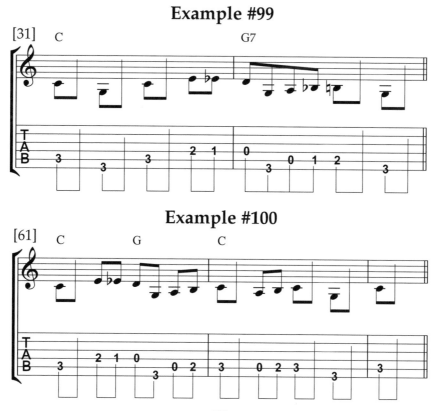

Example #100

Example #101

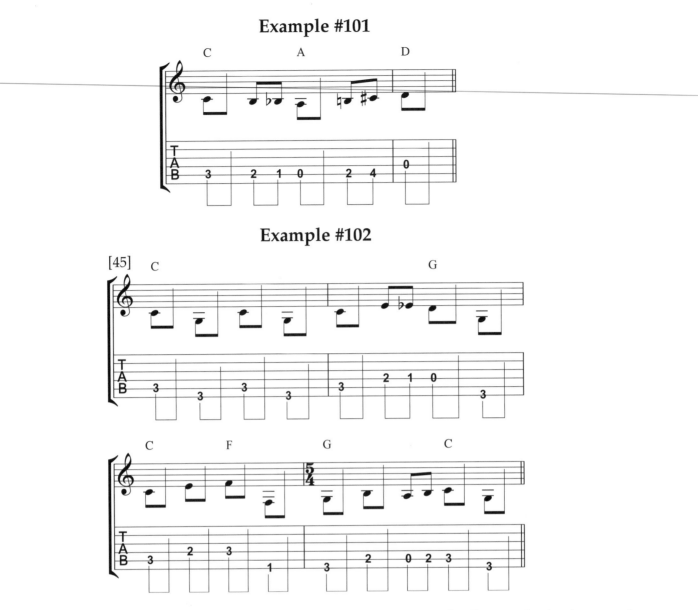

Example #102

Now, let's move to the main entrée of this section: the lick C-D-E flat-E natural. Again, note the flat third-natural third blues note sequence. Once again, here is the basic lick:

Example #103

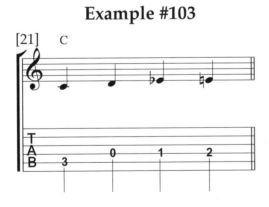

The next four examples demonstrate the lick used as part of a backup pattern:

Example #104

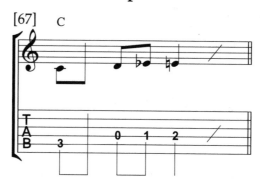

Example #105

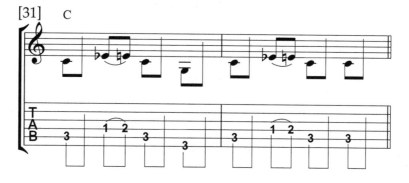

Example #106

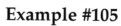

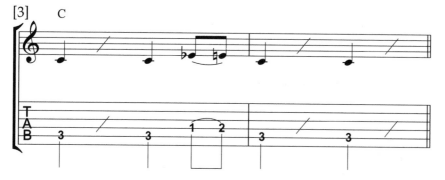

Variation

Example #107

Here is an example of the lick in 3/4 time, in a I-V-I chord progression. The phrase begins with the 5-6-7-8 connector run, which segues into the flat third-natural third note sequence.

Example #108

Let's look at this lick in some standard chord progressions:

I-IV (C-F)

Example #109

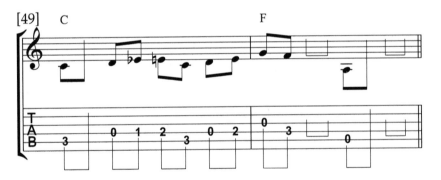

Example #110

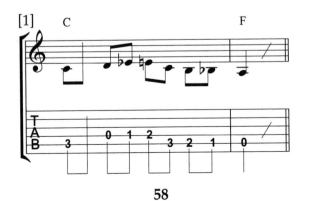

IV-V-I (C-D-G)

Example #111

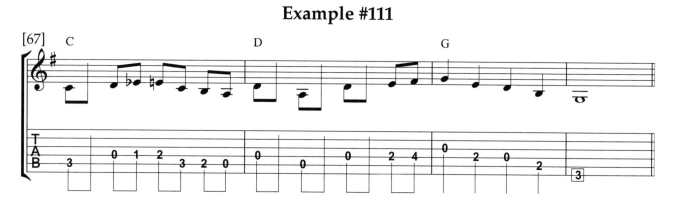

V-1 (G-C)

Example #112

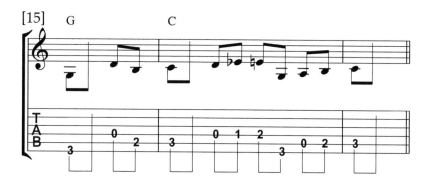

Here is an example of a 5-6 7-8 connector immediately followed by a Root-2nd-flat 3rd-natural 3rd lick. Note the repeat of the root note, C.

Example #113

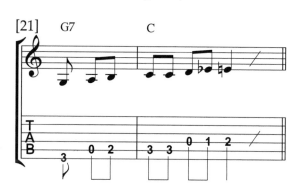

Next is an example of the basic lick followed by a short G-style run:

Example #114

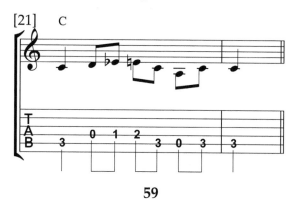

The lick can be repeated as a form of imitation or when chord changes occur:

Example #115

Example #116

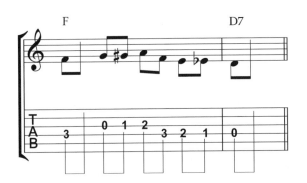

Next are three examples of the lick used in various chord changes:

Example #117

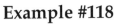

Example #118

Example #119

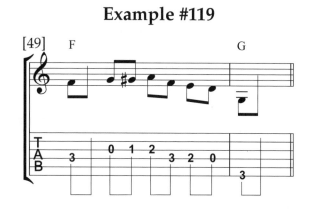

In Example 120 note how the basic phrase resolves to a different chord:

Example #120

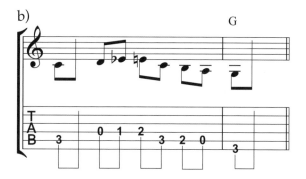

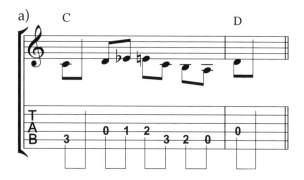

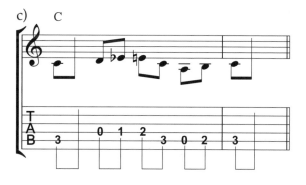

Hopefully, from the examples I have provided here you have seen how useful this lick can be in various contexts. Before we move along, here is a full 8-measure transcription using the lick; note the variations.

Example #121

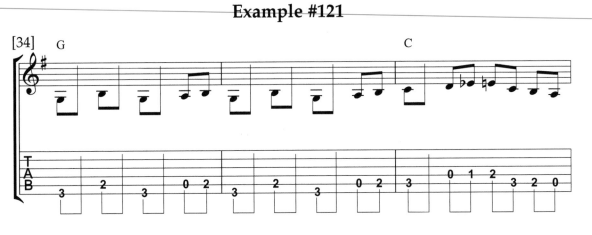

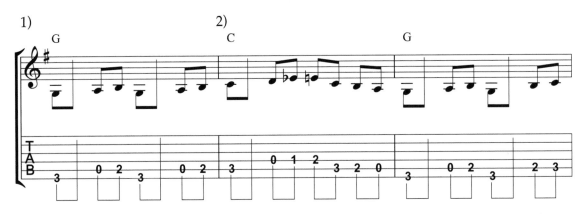

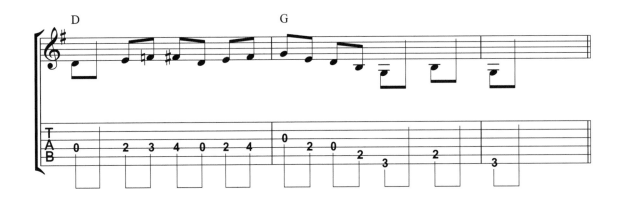

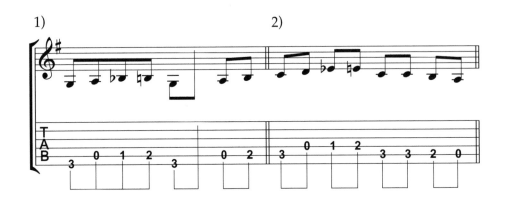

LICKS OVER A CHORD

This section simply provides examples I transcribed from the historic recordings of a wide variety of licks played over a certain chord:

G major:

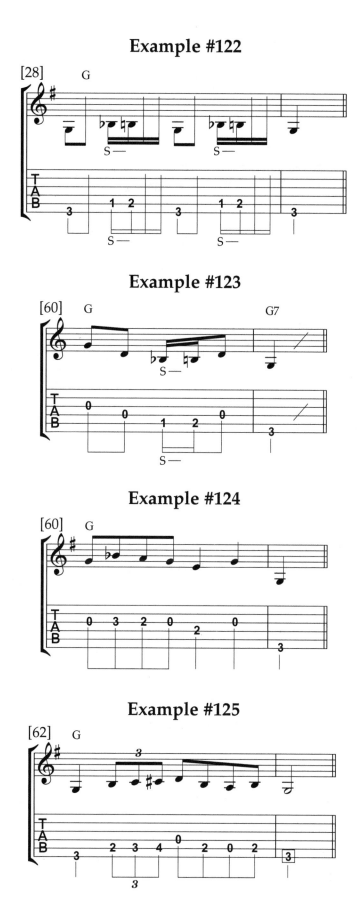

Example #122

Example #123

Example #124

Example #125

Example #126

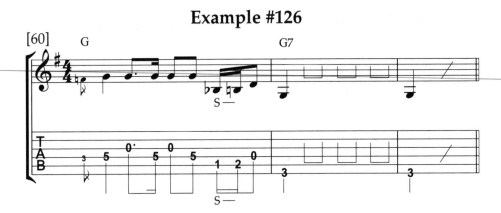

Example #127

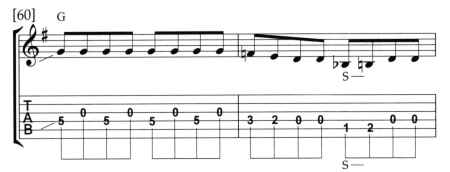

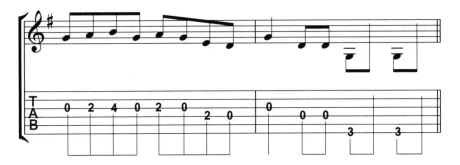

Example #128

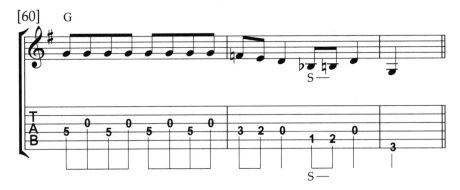

Example #129

Example #130

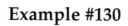
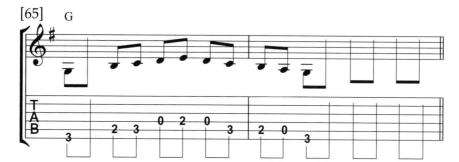
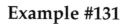

Example #131

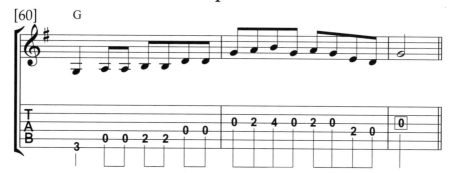

Example #132

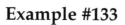

A major:

Example #133

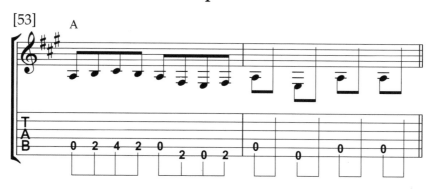

Example #134

Transposed to G:

Example #135

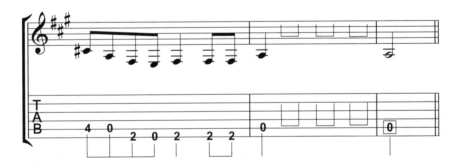

Example #136

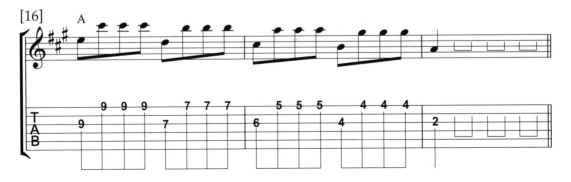

D major:

Example #137

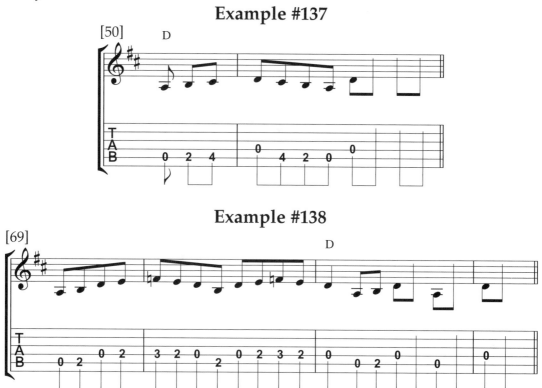

Example #138

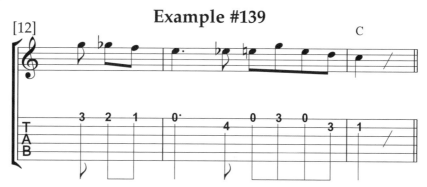

C major:

Example #139

Cannon's Jug Stompers, consisted of Gus Cannon, Ashley Thompson and Noah Lewis.

67

F major:

Example #140

First Opry tour group, 1930. Standing, left to right: Kirk McGee, Dr. Humphrey Bate, Doriiis Macon, Buster Bate, Aclyone Bate, Loe Hesson.   Seated: Sam Mcgee, Uncle Dave Macon.

LICKS OVER A CHORD PROGRESSION

Now, let's look at some more extended licks used over short chord progressions.

I - IV (G-C):

Example #141

IV - I (C-G):

Example #142

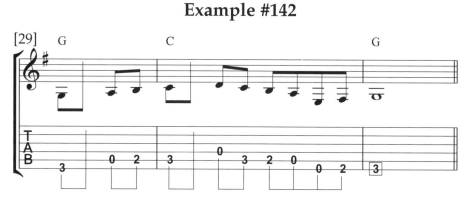

I - V (C-G):

Example #143

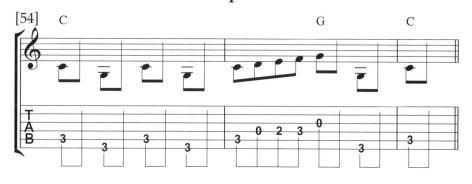

II - V - I (E7-A7-D):

Example #144

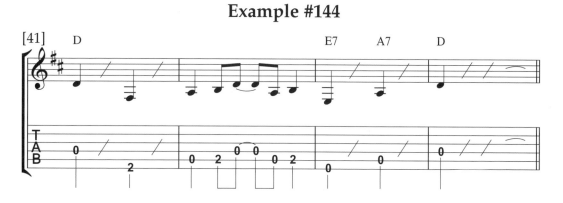

III - VI - II - V - I (B7-E7-A7-D7-G):

Example #145

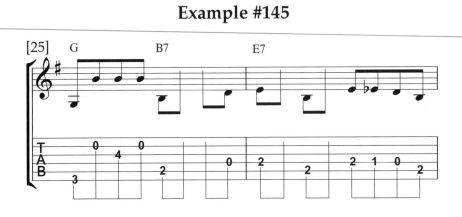

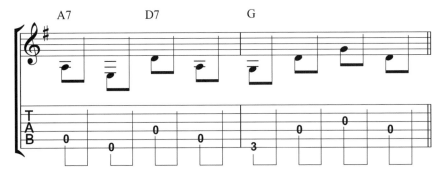

V - I:

Example #146

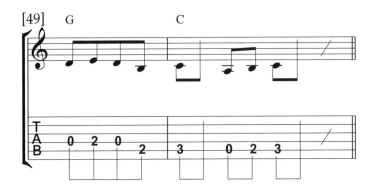

Example #147

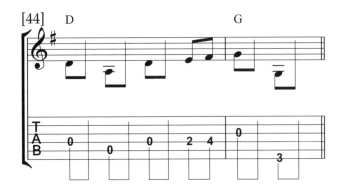

Example #148

Variation

Variation

Example #149

Example #150

Example #151

Example #152

Example #153

Example #154

I think that you now have at your disposal a good variety of authentic licks you can use in your own arrangements. Have fun with them!

16TH NOTE RUNS

You have probably noticed that almost everything presented in this book has been presented using eighth note pairings. Obviously, it is difficult using just your thumb and fingers uses as a unit to develop additional speed. This is not to say that it wasn't done, as the playing of Riley Puckett of Gid Tanner and His Skillet Lickers amply demonstrates.

With this in mind, here is an example of 16th note usage in a pickup note sequence:

Example #155

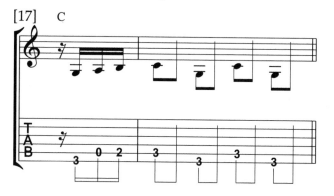

Next are a few examples of standard eighth note bass connectors played as 16th notes:

Example #156

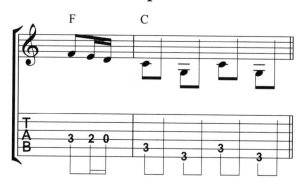

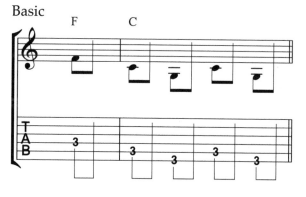

Example #157

Example #158

Example #159

Here are some examples of 16th note usage in slightly longer phrases:

Example #160

Example #161

Example #162

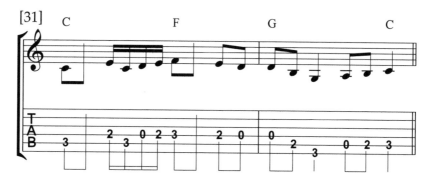

Example #163

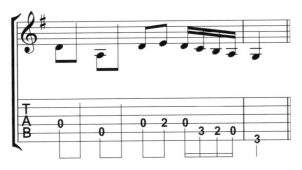

Varied

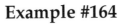

Example #164

Finally, here are a few examples where notes are tied creating a syncopated effect:

Example #165

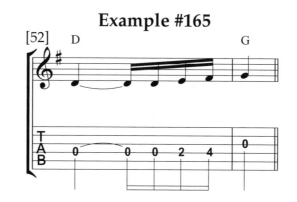

Example #166

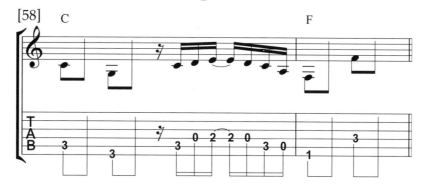

Example #167

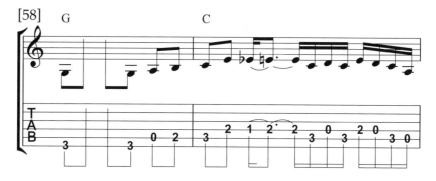

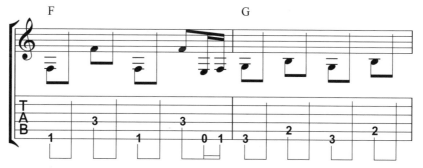

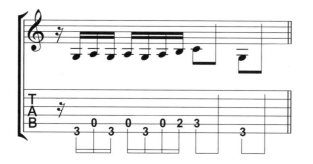

MISCELLANEOUS TECHNIQUES

Hammer-Ons.

I previously mentioned that hammer-ons were not used as frequently as we might suppose, based on contemporary guitar usage of the last 50 years. Here are two examples:

Example #168

Example #169

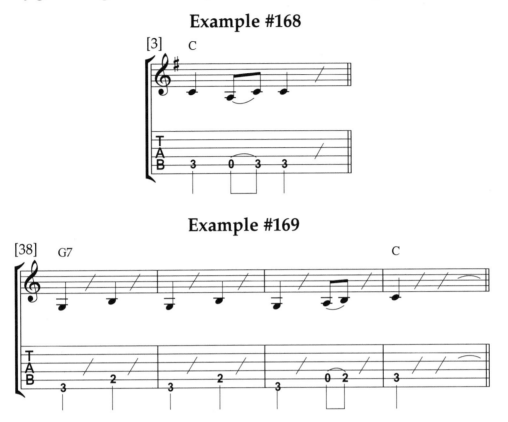

Carter Family Licks.

Here are two examples of Carter Family-style guitar backup:

Example #170

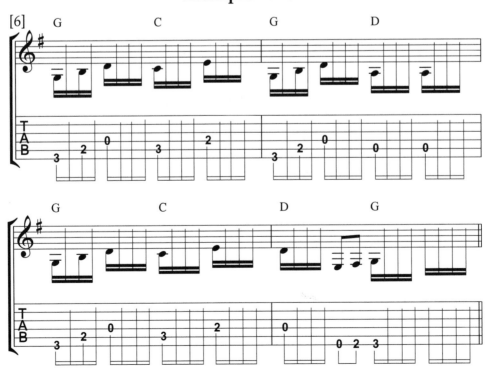

Example #171

Rolls/Arpeggio Patterns.

Here are some examples of how rolls are used on those historic recordings:

Example #172

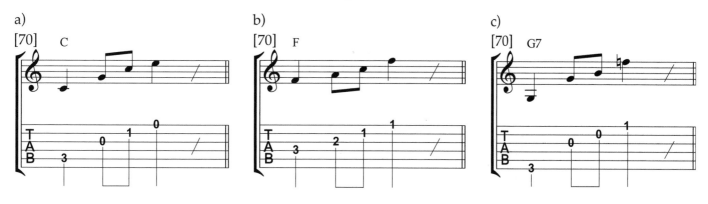

Example #173

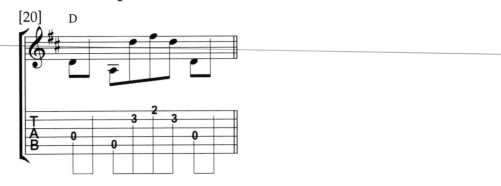

Example #174

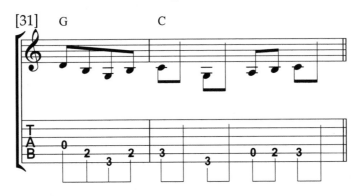

Example #175

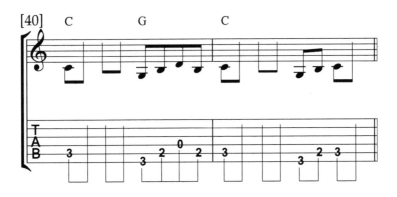

Example #176

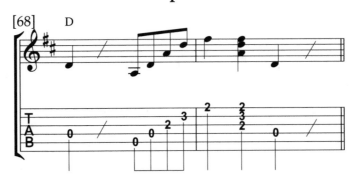

Triplets.

Here is an example of the use of triplets in a blues-style song:

Example #177

Triad.

I think that it would be appropriate to end Part Two with a triadic cadential figure:

Example #178

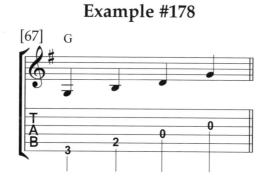

81

EPILOGUE

In your hands you are holding some of the collective wisdom of many string band guitarists, some famous, some not. Their playing represents the guitar performance practice from the Golden Age of commercial recordings of the 1920s and early 1930s. Their backup performances and repertoire laid the foundation, the bedrock, of all that followed in country guitar and bluegrass guitar styles.

For more information on old-time country guitar styles I suggest that you look at my book, *Guitar Backup Styles of Southern String Bands from the Golden Age of Phonograph Recordings*, which features the guitar backup styles of Ernest Stoneman's Dixie Mountaineers (the playing style of Grayson and Whitter is similar to that of Ernest Stoneman), the Carter Family, Charlie Poole and the North Carolina Ramblers, Gid Tanner and the Skillet Lickers, and Jimmie Rodgers, often acknowledged as "the father of country music." These artists are not represented in *Old-Time Country Guitar Backup Basics* because each have unique performance aspects that, while built on the basic back-up patterns covered in Part One of this book, go above and beyond them.

Joseph Weidlich
Washington, DC

The Delmore Brothers, Rabon and Alton.

SONG REFERENCE LIST

1. *A Black Woman is Like A Black Snake*
   Memphis Jug Band

2. *Bamalong Blues*
   Andrew and Jim Baxter

3. *Charleston #1*
   Narmour and Smith

4. *Charley, He's A Good Old Man*
   Kelly Harrell

5. *Charming Bill*
   Sam and Kirk McGee (with Uncle Dave Macon)

6. *Chewing Chewing Gum*
   Lake Howard

7. *Choctaw County Rag*
   Ray Brothers

8. *Cotton Mill Blues*
   Lee Brothers

9. *Daisies Won't Tell*
   Roy Harvey

10. *Darneo*
    Blue Ridge Highballers

11. *Forty Drops*
    Andrew and Jim Baxter

12. *Frisco Town*
    Memphis Minnie

13. *Georgia Crawl*
    Henry Williams and Eddie Anthony

14. *Going to Germany*
    Cannon's Jug Stompers

15. *Goodbye Maggie, Goodbye Darling*
    West Virginia Ramblers

16. *Got the Farm Land Blues*
    Carolina Tar Heels

17. *Got the Jake Leg Too*
    Ray Brothers

18. *The Grape Vine Twist*
    Steve and his Hot Shots

19. *Grave in the Pines*
    Clayton McMichen

20. *How Can A Poor Man Stand Such Times and Live*
    Blind Alfred Reed

21. *How Long*
    Frank Stokes

22. *I Went to See My Sweetheart*
    Lewis McDaniel and Walter Smith

23. *I'll Remember You in My Prayers*
    Blue Ridge Mountain Singers

24. *Jackson Stomp*
    Mississippi Mud Steppers

25. *The Jazz Fiddler*
    Walter Jacobs and Lonnie Carter

26. *Johnson Gal*
    Leake County Revelers

27. *Keno the Rent Man*
    Cofer Brothers

28. *Killin' Blues*
    Byrd Moore and Jess Johnston

29. *Kitty Hill*
    Bill Chitwood and his Georgia Mountaineers

30. *Knocking Down Casey Jones*
    Wilmer Watts and the Lonely Eagles

31. *Little Black Mustache*
    Clardy and Clements

32. *Little Bunch of Roses*
    Murphy Brothers Harp Band

33. *Little Sweetheart Pal of Mine*
    Red Fox Chasers

34. *Lonesome Road Blues*
    Leftwich and Lilly

35. *Look On and Cry*
    Wade Mainer

36. *Louisville Burglar*
    Hickory Nuts

37. *Magnolia Two-Step*
   Nations Brothers

38. *Mississippi Echoes*
   Ray Brothers

39. *Moanin' and Groanin' Blues*
   "Peg Leg" Howell and his Gang

40. *Molly Put the Kettle On*
   Leake County Revelers

41. *Mule Get Up in the Alley*
   Cannon's Jug Stompers

42. *Muskrat Rag*
   Jarvis and Justice

43. *Nine Pound Hammer*
   Frank Blevins and his Tar Heel Rattlers

44. *The Old Hat*
   Leake County Revelers

45. *Old Joe*
   Sid Harkreader and Gradey Moore

46. *Once I Loved A Railroad Flagman*
   Frank Jenkins and his Pilot Mountaineers

47. *Otto Wood the Bandit*
   Carolina Buddies

48. *Polly Put the Kettle On*
   Stoneman's Blue Ridge Cornchuckers

49. *Prison Sorrows*
   Weaver Brothers

50. *Ragtime Annie*
   Corn Cob Crushers

51. *Railroad Blues*
   Roy Harvey

52. *Robertson County*
   Paul Warmack and his Gully Jumpers

53. *Rock House Gamblers*
   Cleve Chaffin and the McClung Brothers

54. *Rock That Cradle Lucy*
   Cofer Brothers

55. *The Rooster's Crowing Blues*
   Cannon's Jug Stompers

56. *Sally Goodin*
   Kessinger Brothers

57. *Starving to Death on a Government Claim*
   Edward L. Crain

58. *Stone Rag*
   Paul Warmack and his Gully Jumpers

59. *Tallapoosa Bound*
   A.A. Gray and Seven Foot Dilly

60. *Teasin' Brown Blues*
   Louis Laskey

61. *Tell It To Me*
   Grant Brothers and Their Music

62. *Them Good Old Times and Coming Back Again*
   Jim Baird

63. *Times is Tight Like That*
   Bo Carter and Walter Vinson

64. *Tired of You Driving Me*
   Memphis Jug Band

65. *Warfield*
   Williamson Brothers and Curry

66. *What Will I Do For My Money's All Gone*
   Eck Dunford and Hattie Stoneman

67. *When the Bees are in the Hive*
   Roy Harvey

68. *You Are My Sunshine*
   Wif Carter

69. *You Shall*
   Frank Stokes and Dane Sane

70. *You'll Miss Me*
   Alfred and Orville Reed

Other Guitar Books by Centerstream Publishing LLC.
P.O. Box 17878 - Anaheim Hills, CA 92807
email: centerstrm@aol.com

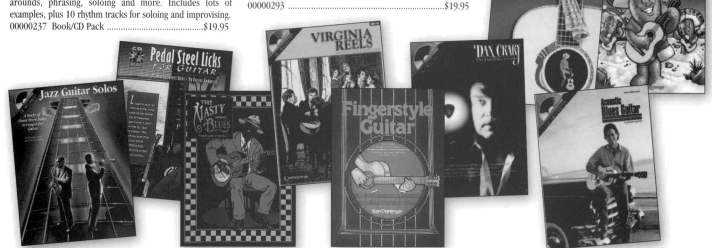

GUITAR INSTRUCTION & TECHNIQUE

GUITAR CHORDS PLUS
by Ron Middlebrook
A comprehensive study of normal and extended chords, tuning, keys, transposing, capo use, and more. Includes over 500 helpful photos and diagrams, a key to guitar symbols, and a glossary of guitar terms.
00000011..$11.95

GUITAR TUNING FOR THE COMPLETE MUSICAL IDIOT (FOR SMART PEOPLE TOO)
by Ron Middlebrook

A complete book on how to tune up. Contents include: Everything You Need To Know About Tuning; Intonation; Strings; 12-String Tuning; Picks; and much more.
00000002 ....$5.95

INTRODUCTION TO ROOTS GUITAR
by Doug Cox

This book/CD pack by Canada's premier guitar and Dobro® player introduces beginning to intermediate players to many of the basics of folk/roots guitar. Topics covered include: basic theory, tuning, reading tablature, right- and left-hand patterns, blues rhythms, Travis picking, frailing patterns, flatpicking, open tunings, slide and many more. CD includes 40 demonstration tracks.
00000262 Book/CD Pack $17.95
00000265 VHS Video................................$19.95

KILLER PENTATONICS FOR GUITAR
by Dave Celentano

Covers innovative and diverse ways of playing pentatonic scales in blues, rock and heavy metal. The licks and ideas in this book will give you a fresh approach to playing the pentatonic scale, hopefully inspiring you to reach for higher levels in your playing. The 37-minute companion CD features recorded examples.
00000285 Book/CD Pack $17.95

LEFT HAND GUITAR CHORD CHART
by Ron Middlebrook
Printed on durable card stock, this "first-of-a-kind" guitar chord chart displays all forms of major and minor chords in two forms, beginner and advanced.
00000005..$2.95

MELODIC LINES FOR THE INTERMEDIATE GUITARIST
by Greg Cooper
This book/CD pack is essential for anyone interested in expanding melodic concepts on the guitar. Author Greg Cooper covers: picking exercises; major, minor, dominant and altered lines; blues and jazz turn-arounds; and more.
00000312 Book/CD Pack $19.95

MELODY CHORDS FOR GUITAR
by Allan Holdsworth
Influential fusion player Allan Holdsworth provides guitarists with a simplified method of learning chords, in diagram form, for playing accompaniments and for playing popular melodies in "chord-solo" style. Covers: major, minor, altered, dominant and diminished scale notes in chord form, with lots of helpful reference tables and diagrams.
00000222..$19.95

MODAL JAMS AND THEORY
by Dave Celentano
This book shows you how to play the modes, the theory behind mode construction, how to play any mode in any key, how to play the proper mode over a given chord progression, and how to write chord progressions for each of the seven modes. The CD includes two rhythm tracks and a short solo for each mode so guitarists can practice with a "real" band.
00000163 Book/CD Pack $17.95

MONSTER SCALES AND MODES
by Dave Celentano
This book is a complete compilation of scales, modes, exotic scales, and theory. It covers the most common and exotic scales, theory on how they're constructed, and practical applications. No prior music theory knowledge is necessary, since every section is broken down and explained very clearly.
00000140..$7.95

OPEN GUITAR TUNINGS
by Ron Middlebrook
This booklet illustrates over 75 different tunings in easy-to-read diagrams. Includes tunings used by artists such as Chet Atkins, Michael Hedges, Jimmy Page, Joe Satriani and more for rock, blues, bluegrass, folk and country styles including open D (for slide guitar), Em, open C, modal tunings and many more.
00000130..$4.95

OPEN TUNINGS FOR GUITAR
by Dorian Michael

This book provides 14 folk songs in 9 tunings to help guitarists become comfortable with changing tunings. Songs are ordered so that changing from one tuning to another is logical and non-intrusive. Includes: Fisher Blues (DADGBE) • Fine Toast to Hewlett (DGDGBE) • George Barbazan (DGDGBD) • Amelia (DGDGCD) • Will the Circle Be Unbroken (DADF#AD) • more.
00000224 Book/CD Pack $19.95

ARRANGING FOR OPEN GUITAR TUNINGS
By Dorian Michael
This book/CD pack teaches intermediate-level guitarists how to choose an appropriate tuning for a song, develop an arrangement, and solve any problems that may arise while turning a melody into a guitar piece to play and enjoy.
00000313 Book/CD Pack $19.95

ROCK RHYTHM GUITAR
by Dave Celentano
This helpful book/CD pack cuts out all the confusing technical talk and just gives guitarists the essential tools to get them playing. With Celentano's tips, anyone can build a solid foundation of basic skills to play almost any rhythm guitar style. The exercises and examples are on the CD, in order of difficulty, so players can master new techniques, then move on to more challenging material.
00000274 Book/CD Pack $17.95

SCALES AND MODES IN THE BEGINNING
by Ron Middlebrook

The most comprehensive and complete scale book written especially for the guitar. Chapers include: Fretboard Visualization • Scale Terminology • Scales and Modes • and a Scale to Chord Guide.
00000010 ....$11.95

SLIDE GUITAR AND OPEN TUNINGS
by Doug Cox
Explores the basics of open tunings and slide guitar for the intermediate player, including licks, chords, songs and patterns. This is not just a repertoire book, but rather an approach for guitarists to jam with others, invent their own songs, and understand how to find their way around open tunings with and without a slide. The accompanying CD features 37 tracks.
00000243 Book/CD Pack $17.95

SPEED METAL
by Dave Celentano
In an attempt to teach the aspiring rock guitarist how to pick faster and play more melodically, Dave Celentano uses heavy metal neo-classical styles from Paganini and Bach to rock in this great book/CD pack. The book is structured to take the player through the examples in order of difficulty.
00000261 Book/CD Pack $17.95

25 WAYS TO IMPROVE YOUR SOLO GUITAR PLAYING *NEW*
by Jay Marks
Keep your music fresh with the great ideas in this new book! Covers: chords, dynamics, harmonics, phrasing, intros & endings and more!
00000323 Book/CD Pack $19.95